Oh, Mama

BY JAN WATKINS

Cover photograph and inside photographs
taken from the Sutphin and Wright family collections
and the private collection of Jan Watkins.
Back cover photo by Jackie Girard,
Photographer, Defense Supply Center Richmond.

ISBN 978-0-615-23441-0

MANUFACTURED AND PRINTED IN THE
UNITED STATES OF AMERICA

First Edition

For my friends Joyce, Alice and Jean. Joyce, who has been a best friend since we met at Longwood University in 1960—Alice, who loves me like only Alice can love—Jean, who listened to my stories for years and encouraged me to write them down. To all of you, I have written the book as if I were telling you.

And for Sydney and Albert. Perhaps you will tell some of these stories to your grandchildren.

Acknowledgements

My thanks to Maude Kerby, Chesterfield Book Exchange, Midlothian, Virginia, and Barbara Fandrich, Editor, Centralia, Washington, for reading the manuscript and offering their opinions. Thanks also to those who shared their stories of Mama and Daddy with me.

3/5/09

Barbara,

I believe Mama would be proud. Thank you for your part.

Jan

Notes

The material in italics was taken from interviews with my brother Harless, Mama's sisters Geneva, Snowa, Christine and Phyllis, and Mama's friends Nell and Margie.

A Name Guide is in the back of the book.

All misspelled words or misused grammar is intentional.

His Eye is on the Sparrow

Whenever I am tempted, whenever clouds arise,
When songs give place to sighing, when hope within me dies,
I draw the closer to Him, from care He sets me free,
His eye is on the sparrow, and I know He watches me.

Civilla D. Martin, 1866-1948

Preface

And so it begins. The writing of The Book about Mama. Mama died in 2001 at age eighty-one and the stories and memories began to surface, but I put off writing them down until I retired.

During the days and weeks after her death, we felt our loss profoundly. It hurt to even look at her picture. As each day passed we began to go through her things and over and over, the phrase Oh, Mama would come to my mind. When I first came across something in her handwriting, it brought me to my knees. And then there was Daddy, who was difficult at best. In his state of dementia that we hadn't yet identified, he was impossible. And again the phrase came to my mind, Oh, Mama. What you had to live through. What you had to endure. The sacrifices you had to make on account of your children. And so I realized that had to be the title of this book.

It is now November 2003. Daddy died in March. I am now retired and living in a cottage which I have rented for the winter on the Outer Banks of North Carolina, with the ocean at my door and the noisy seagulls overhead, being able to afford it only because of Mama and Daddy and their lifetime of saving and the money they left me. Thank you, Mama. Thank you, Daddy.

I woke up happy this morning, thinking about Mama, knowing that today I would begin. I turned on the coffee, made the bed and sat down to write. All the chores have been done, all the errands have been run. The firewood is laid in for the winter and there is no more reason for procrastinating. I am anxious to get started and scared to death at the same time. Scared that I won't do it right. Wanting so badly to write a story that will do her justice, honor her name.

Jan Watkins
Outer Banks
November 2003

Chapter 1

Last Day

I wish that I had been able to get down on my knees beside her chair the day before she died and tell her how much I loved her. To tell her not to be afraid because I felt that death would be peaceful. To tell her she had been the best of mothers and we all loved her so much. But speaking about love or even hugging wasn't part of her demeanor. I cannot remember her ever coming up to me and hugging me. When we had Christmas at my house, one of the rituals I started was everyone hugged before sitting down to eat. She liked that we did that. Outside of that, she had never been one to show very much physical closeness. It had always been that way.

After behaving a certain way with her all of my life, it wasn't possible for me to change it now, here in our family's home, where all us kids had become teenagers, adults, married, moved away, had children of our own whom we brought back to this family home, where they came to know and love her as we did, grandchildren who got lots of hugs. And I smiled when it happened because I understood.

I didn't know anything about what happened when someone died. I had never known anyone close to me who had died. I had never been in anyone's presence while they were dying. We knew that she didn't have long to live but I couldn't bring myself to say what I was thinking. The knowledge that she was dying brought such an ache in my chest that I couldn't get around it. All I could do was rub her arm or her knee as she sat there in her famous recliner and put on a brave face and choke back the tears. How stupid we are to try to be strong. Who started that ridiculous practice anyway. Be strong in the face of death. Don't let them know that they actually might be dying. Don't sob your heart out and clutch onto her like you want to. I have regretted it every day of my life since.

But if I had been truly strong, I would have said I don't know if this is your time to go or not. But just in case, I want to tell you some things. I want to tell you how much we love you. You are our anchor, our friend, our confidant. I wouldn't take a million dollars for the times you and I spent together traveling. I know that made you happy. It made me happy too. I'm so glad we did that. You did right by all of us. I hope we did right by you. I'm sorry for all the times I let you down. You always showed us the right and Christian way to live. I'll try to keep that up. I'll try to keep making you proud of me. I know you're afraid. I wish you wouldn't be. I think you just go to sleep. I think it must be peaceful. Oh, Mama.

Chapter 2

Mama Was Born in the Blue Ridge Mountains

*W*e knew she was an above-average mother, an above-average person. But after she died and we had to take care of Daddy, we decided she must have been a saint. They had been married sixty-two years when Mama died.

Mama was born in Floyd County, Virginia in October 1919 in a drafty old house, the third of nine children to Salina Katheryn (called Cass or Cassie) and Elmond Sutphin. There were two daughters before her, and five daughters and two sons after her: Myrtle, Virginia, Beulah Mae (who was Mama), Geneva, Baby Girl (stillborn), Fred, Christine, Snowa, Rush (nicknamed Bud), and Phyllis. She was born into a life of hard times and no luxuries. Floyd County is in the Blue Ridge Mountains of Virginia and there was barely enough money to get by. Everything was homemade and homegrown. Elmond was a carpenter by trade. He was a really tall, big-boned, lanky man, stooping to go through doorways. He was very religious and was a member of the Pentecostal Holiness Church.

Cass was also tall and big-boned and possessed what I later named the Sutphin fat gene. We called her Big Granny. There were few pictures of Big Granny when my mother was young, but the few in existence showed her as weighing at least 250 pounds. We loved Big Granny being big. She was soft and warm and could cook like no one else.

Mama went to school in Floyd County, but was only able to finish the sixth grade. The life she described in stories she told us about growing up in Floyd County was one of attending a one-room schoolhouse, sleeping several to a bed in a loft, and having snow blow through the crack in the logs at her head where she was sleeping. Eight of the nine children were born there, in the house that had only one large room downstairs and a loft upstairs where the children slept. Many of Mama's stories would begin "During the Depression..." She was referring to the Great Depression of 1929-1939 which gripped all of America during the time of her childhood and early adulthood, but especially hard hit were those people who lived in the bone-chilling raw land of the Blue Ridge Mountains of Virginia. If you went anywhere at all, it was in a wagon pulled by a horse.

Aunt Snowa tells of the time when she was born in March 1932. Snow was in drifts up to seven feet. When Big Granny went into labor, Granddaddy had to hitch up the horse and go for the doctor. They had to take the quilts off of the beds to wrap around Granddaddy. Mama and the other children had to sleep in the loft that night in their coats because Granddaddy had all the quilts. The horse would get lodged in the snow up to his legs and Granddaddy would have to dig him out. That's how Snowa came to have her name. Big Granny cried all night because she didn't know if Granddaddy would make it back. Granddaddy put the doctor on his horse and brought him back. Big Granny almost died from loss of blood. There was no mail for six weeks.

Mama and her sisters went to school sporadically and Mama managed to learn to read and count. She read everything there was to read but there wasn't much. Any reading was done at night by kerosene lamps and one time she and her sisters made younger brother Fred lie on his back on the bed and hold the lamp on his stomach to give them light. They were supposed to be asleep so this was all done in secret. They kept this up for so long that Fred got burns on his belly and Mama and her sisters got a beating from Big Granny.

All of Mama's sisters told me that Big Granny favored Uncle Fred and paid him special attention. They said Big Granny coddled him because she had waited so long for a boy. And Mama and her sisters were jealous of him because of it. Mama told about another time when Big Granny and Granddaddy were out in the fields working. They left Fred at home and told the sisters to mind him. Fred pestered them constantly and finally tiring of him, they took off all his clothes and locked him in a cold room. He almost caught pneumonia and Mama got a whipping because she was the instigator. There couldn't have been a tighter bond, though, as the girls and Fred and Bud grew up and married. Fred was always the jokester and the one who teased the cousins and the boyfriends of all the nieces. Once when I brought a date to the family reunion, Fred told him he wasn't near as ugly as I had said. He also told my daughter Wendy when she brought her boyfriend to the reunion that he didn't look at all like the last guy she brought. One of his most-told stories to nieces and nephews with freckles was that their freckles got there because a cow had coughed while chewing her cud and had spewed bran all over their faces and it stuck. The kids would look at each other and the other adults to see if they should believe him. Eventually somebody would laugh though and give it away.

Elmond and Cass and their eight children moved from Floyd County to a four-room house on First Street in Radford, Virginia in 1934 when Mama was fifteen. Because of Granddaddy's religion and strict rules, none of the seven daughters was allowed to go out on dates with boys in cars or allowed to wear makeup or allowed to dance. They were not allowed to wear pants, only skirts or dresses. Courting took place in the living room and on the swing on the front porch under the watchful and sanctimonious eye of Elmond. Fred, who was about ten, would hide in the closet in the front room and watch while they courted. When she was about seventeen, Mama got a job in the shirt factory in Radford. She and her older sister Virginia both worked in the shirt factory and all of their earnings were given to Big Granny and Granddaddy. She was working at the shirt factory when she met my father, Posey Harless Wright. Mama was eighteen, Daddy was twenty-four. At the time, he had hair, but it would be gone by the time he was twenty-five. They married in January 1938, about three months after they met.

Daddy was born in Carroll County, Virginia, which was next door to Floyd County, on October 15, 1913 to John William and Florence Wright. There were twelve children in all, seven boys and five girls, born in this order: Rozzel, Kale, Earl, Annie, Laura, Posey, Harding, Dorothy, William, Gladys, Dolly and Henry. Grandpa Wright was known only to me as Grandpa Wright. Neighbors or friends would call him Mr. Wright, but I never heard anyone ever call him by his given name, John. He was handsome, jolly, about five feet ten inches tall and sturdy. He was a farmer all of his life and when Daddy was born, they lived in a small house up in a "holler." A holler is a hollow, pronounced holler by country people, and is an area of land between two mountains where homes were sometimes built on the side of the mountain or if you were lucky, in the small flat space at the convergence of the two mountains; mountain spring runoff usually took the route of the hollers on their way to the ocean and provided good bottomland for grazing and farming, if you could get rid of the rocks. Living in the hills of Virginia was a hardscrabble life, isolated from most of society, children with little schooling and mountain ways handed down from one generation to the next.

Daddy's mother, Florence, was short and small and wore her gray hair wound in a bun on the back of her head. She appeared to be delicate. She was the only person I can ever recall Mama saying anything bad about. Mama didn't like her very much. Mama said she was mean. She said Florence taught her children to be mean too. Especially the boys. Mean as in they would steal something in a heartbeat and Florence would praise them when they got away with it. I don't remember much about her except that she had a stern face, wore glasses with no frames, and was short and thin. She died of a stroke in 1951 at about age sixty-two when I was nine. I don't remember much about her funeral except that I remember Daddy's chin quivering as he fought back tears. That was the first time I had ever seen Daddy cry. I think the next time was on my wedding day.

Daddy was named Posey Harless, which were names used only in the Appalachian hills. He sometimes spelled his name Posie, and although now it seems strange that he spelled his name two different ways, it didn't seem strange at all to us kids when we were growing up. I think he didn't know how to spell his name and sometimes got it confused. Because his name conjured up a vision of a flower with most people, he endured teasing about his name all of his life. He didn't pay it much mind though. His birth date was questionable as well. He was middle-aged before Mama inspected his birth certificate and discovered he was actually born late at night on October 14. We continued to celebrate his birthday on October 15, just as before.

**Interview with Mama's sister Geneva,
August 2004 at the Sutphin home on First Street in Radford:**

I remember when we's a courtin', me and Beulah Mae would be in here (pointing to the living room) *and Posey would come and I remember William* (William was Daddy's younger brother) *used to come, I used to court William a little bit and they would both come and we would be in the living room. We had a closet right here and Fred would get in that closet and peek through them cracks in there to us. He was always doing something, he follered us everywhere we went, Fred did. But I remember we had an old Victrola, and we'd crank that thing and listen to records. We'd play records while we talked. And Dad used to get up, we'd set up' til late at night, and he would go to bed early. Him and Mommy was in that other room in the front bedroom. And he would get up. They had a stove in there, in the corner of the wall, and Dad would get up and pee in the pot and he'd shake the grate in the stove so that we couldn't hear him pee.*

When we were courting, we used to sit out on the front porch in the swing with our boyfriends. I remember Posey didn't have no hind end. There wasn't very many cars. Daddy told us not to never get in a car with nobody. He'd make me go with Beulah Mae everywhere she went. I would go walking with them when Beulah Mae was on a date. They would go on ahead of us walking and I would stay way behind them. We walked everwhere.

One time we was going up the road here going to prayer meeting up on the hill and I told her I didn't know where babies come from and I was twelve years old I guess, and I never had heard anything in school or nothing and I asked her. We was going up here about Third Street. And I asked her where babies come from and she told me and that just shocked me. I couldn't believe that that was where babies come from.

After Beulah Mae and Posey married, they moved into a farmhouse on some land bordering the New River which runs through Radford, Virginia. Daddy ran the farm and planted corn crops and raised cattle and pigs. It was called Flannigan's Farm. They were allowed to live in the house for free as part of Daddy's pay for running the farm. Three years later, in 1941, my brother Harless was born in that farmhouse, followed by me in 1942. By the time my sister Doris was born in 1943, the doctor had convinced Daddy that any more children would have to be born in the hospital, not at home. Mama had endured a long labor with my brother and me, and the farmhouse was a long ways from town. As Mama told it, Dr. Geisen put his foot down and said it was too hard on Mama and the doctor to go through another home birth. Mama recalled that the hospital cost $25 and Daddy had not wanted to put out that much money. Dr. Geisen said he would knock $5 off the bill if Daddy would take Mama to the hospital for Doris' birth and so he did. Sister Nancy was born in 1945, also in the hospital.

Interview with Mama's sister Snowa,
August 2004 at her home in Salem, Virginia:

What I remember most was when one of you kids was born and Posey would take Beulah to the hospital and Mother was keeping the little ones and he would come up there and cry like a baby and Mother would say that he was the most tender-hearted person. And he would never let you kids move and if he brought y'all up there you was not allowed out of your seat. But there's a vivid picture in my mind of all you children sitting in a chair in the living room and if one of you would get down he would put you right back and we'd get so aggravated with him because we thought he was too strict on y'all and y'all were the best behaved kids in this world.

My earliest memories of Big Granny and Granddaddy were in that house on First Street in Radford. The house was heated by a pot-bellied stove that Granddaddy kept blazing hot in the corner of the bedroom where Big Granny stayed. It would be cold in all of the other rooms away from the fire, but almost unbearably hot in the room where the stove was. Granddaddy had run water into the house and there was an old claw foot bathtub for bathing. There wasn't much hot water so that when you got into the tub, the sides of the tub would still be cold so you didn't touch the side of the tub while you were washing.

Big Granny cooked on a wood stove in the kitchen and she cooked country food, like pork ribs cooked in a big pot on the back of the stove, cooked until the meat fell off the bone and you ate it on pancakes for breakfast with the greasy juice poured on top. It was one of Daddy's and my favorite dishes. Even when an electric stove was put in the kitchen, Big Granny continued to cook on the wood stove most of the time. She made fresh biscuits or corn pone for every meal. Mama's sister Geneva never married and spent her life taking care of Big Granny and Granddaddy in that house.

Granddaddy died in 1961 and Big Granny died in 1973. Aunt Geneva stayed on, living alone in the house on First Street after Big Granny died. She retired from Burlington Mills in 1986 after forty-three years. She died there on First Street in December 2007 at age eighty-six. Fred, Myrtle, and Virginia have also passed away. As this book is being completed, Mama's siblings Christine, Snowa (along with Uncle Paul), Phyllis (along with Uncle Herbert) and Bud (along with Aunt Nancy) all live in the surrounding area of Radford, Virginia near the house on First Street. Our beloved Aunt Edith who was married to Fred still lives there on First Street as well.

Chapter 3

Flannigan's Farm

Mama and Daddy lived in the farmhouse on Flannigan's Farm until about 1947. I don't remember much about living there but Mama told us about giving birth to my brother Harless and me in that farmhouse. Mama was in labor with me for a couple of days and her sister Virginia came to help and Dr. Geisen would come and go during her labor. Daddy pretty much walked the floor. Mama didn't have a washing machine and had to wash out diapers by hand and hang them on a clothesline. Daddy was out all day working the farm and Mama stayed at home. She gave us a piece of cone pone to chew on when we were teething.

She already knew how to sew and she made dresses for us girls. The only significant memory I have of that time was when a wart that I had on my knee was knocked off when I fell down and I saved it to show to Daddy when he got home. I was running down the walkway to show him as he was pulling up in the car and dropped it and the dog snatched it off the ground and ate it.

Mama told us another story that happened while they were living on Flannigan's Farm about Uncle Fred driving Daddy home in his pickup truck and Daddy was eating a banana. Daddy was very, very particular about his food being clean and he had a very weak stomach. While they were riding along, Fred broke wind and Daddy held his banana out the window until they got home and he could eat it.

Interview with Mama's sister Snowa,
August 2004 at her home in Salem, Virginia:

When y'all were living on Flannigan's Farm, Mother sent me over to your house many times. I guess the reason she sent me so much was because there was always some blackberries or beans to pick and I can't remember picking anything but I remember keeping you kids while they were in the garden. I think that Christine went with me sometimes and I believe Christine would go out in the fields and gather the stuff but that's the only reason I can think that Mother sent me over there and I went time and time again and stayed two or three days at a time. And I remember Beulah Mae coming in in the dark and it was hard for me to get used to fixing the lamps. There was no electricity and lighting the lamps for us to eat supper by and she had that old wood stove for cooking and we was eating by lamplight and of course no bathrooms. I remember one time Posey came through the house naked and probably forgot that I was even there. And I went oops.

We had a big dog named Butter who was part Labrador Retriever. We got Butter when Harless was really young and when

Fred came back from the service, he came over to Flannigan's Farm and started throwing Harless up in the air and Harless started laughing and screaming and Butter bit Fred in the butt. Say that three times real fast.

Harless remembered going to first grade on Flannigan's Farm, a two-room school, there were three grades, outside toilet, four holes in the toilet. He remembered wanting to try on a dirty word he had heard and going into the johnnyhouse with another older boy, tried it on this boy. The boy was real quick to tell him that it was an ugly word, don't say that word, that's a bad word. Harless said he learned a lesson that day about bad words that stuck with him.

Harless carried water in a quart jar to school. Mama put some twine around the top of the jar to make it easier to carry, because he had to carry his books in his arms. One day, probably trying to impress some little girl, he started swinging the jar around and around and the twine came loose and the jar came shooting out and hit a rock and that was the end of his water. Harless said he learned another valuable lesson from that.

During the time that Mama and Daddy lived on Flannigan's Farm, Fred went into the Marines. Mama wrote to Fred while he was in the service and her letters, during the summer of 1944 and winter of 1945, were saved by Fred in an old trunk along with some other memorabilia from the war, and were given to me by Aunt Edith after Fred died in September 2003. Mama mailed the letters with a three-cent stamp.

May 18, 1944
Radford, Virginia

Private Iford F. Sutphin
555-3253 Platoon 275-13BN
Recruit Depot Marine Barracks
Paris Island, South Carolina

Dearest Fred.

I can't find anything to write with but a carpenters pencil so here goes. I got a letter from you yesterday. It was the second I'd got from you. Doris is sick. We took her to the doctor. She's better today. Dr. Geisen said it was because she was cutting teeth. Well we finally got our electricity last week or did I tell you that already. We've been trying to get us a frigidaire but haven't had any luck. We went over home Mon. nite. Our barn burned up while we was gone.

Mama tells me you've decided to be a mechanic but you mentioned something in your other letter about having a rifle. What would a mechanic do with a rifle. Bet you just told her that to keep her from worrying about you. Wish I could be out there with you and help with some of them eats. Our garden is so full of weeds you can't tell which way the rows go. Its rained about every day for a week.

If you can't read this don't blame me to much my pencil is about 1/2 inch wide and 1 inch long.

With love, Beulah Mae

June 28, 1944
Radford, Virginia

Pvt Iford F. Sutphin
Paris Island, South Carolina

Dearest Fred,

It's been a long time since I wrote you but I've had so much to do. We've been trying to gather a few cherries. I've canned 31 quarts and made some jelly. I bet 50 gal. went to waste, we couldn't get time to gather them. Well my frigidaire sure is helpful, couldn't do without it now. Harless and Janet are fighting over the rabbits. I bought them two from Buddy. Glad you enjoyed the books. Will get you some more when I get to go to East end. Got so you can't hardly buy them at Hedges. If theres any particular kind you like please write and tell me. Sure hope you get your furlough. We went to the mill last week at New River. I went to watch the old woman and Posey watched the old man. They stole about a bushel last time. Well I finally bought Katherine's sewing machine. You know I borrowed it away back in the winter. She sold it to me for $35.00. I think I got a bargain. Guess I'd better close. I got two more letters to write and bunch of work to do in the garden. Write real soon and all the news.

Love, Beulah Mae

September 4, 1944
Radford, Virginia

Dearest Fred,

I guess you thought I never would write but I haven't had but two letters from you in a coons age. I've been very busy what with canning and everything else to do. Posey been helping fill silos for some time and I have most everything to do. Its been so darned cold here. It would freeze horns off a brass monkey almost.

We had two squirrels for dinner today. Posey went the other day and killed one and he thinks he has to go every day, since he's going again tonite. I don't get to shoot at anything but hawks. They're catching all our chickens. Well Fred I planned on sending you some books but I couldn't get but three. I went to all the stores. They have lots of true stories and mystery fiction but I didn't know whether you liked to read them or not. Please write and tell me. I stop now. Harless wants to write. Ans. a real long letter.

With love, Beulah Mae

(on the next page were a bunch of squiggly marks; at the top it says from Harless)

October 3, 1944
Radford, Virginia

Pvt Iford F. Sutphin
Cherry Point, North Carolina

Dearest Fred.

I guess you thought I never would write but here goes. How are you? From what Mama tells me about your weight, I expect you to save me your uniforms, after this war is over I'll borrow them. I told you you'd better go light on that ice cream but you wouldn't listen.

Janet got up this morning with a catch in her neck she can't turn her head at all. She's hollered all morning. I weaned Doris the other day and she ain't never stopped howling since so if you hear some kind of ringing in your ears it won't surprise me none. They have just about killed me.

It rained Friday so Posey helped Mrs. Flanagan make kraut in the morning and when he came home at twelve o'clock and told me he didn't have to work in the evening I made him make a crock full for me. He got one day off about two weeks ago to make apple butter, about 12 o'clock it begin pouring down rain he had to build a cover over the kettle. We let it burn a little and the stir we was using come all to pieces in the apple butter, its full of chunks of wood. I'm going to send you a gal. of it for Christmas. Glad you liked the chinkeypens. Sorry I couldn't get but a few. We're going over home tonite to take Mama some chickens. I think she wants some in case Dad invites a half dozen preachers some time to dinner. Looks to me like its about time for you to have another furlough leave or something. Mama waits and watches every week end. She says I just know he'll be here every week end. She says it every Sat nite so why not surprise her sometime. I just gotta close. I can think of nothing to write. Please ans. real soon.

With love, Beulah Mae

February 7, 1945
Radford, Virginia

Pvt Fred Sutphin
Cherry Point, N.C.

Dearest Fred,

I'm almost ashamed to write after so long a time. I just haven't got to it. Got a letter from you Sat. saying you had a strip (so hello General). Its been some of the worst weather here for a bit. So cold I had to bring my canned fruit in by the fire, it froze solid. In case you're interested we're getting about 26 eggs a day. Posey has bought 3 pigs and old Rose was fresh the other day. I guess Ma wrote you about Posey having some trouble with his leg. Well its almost well now but he mashed his thumb almost off the other day. I shudder to think which part of his body will be the next victim. He and Harless are shucking corn over on the hill now. Well I'll have to stop. We're going over home tonite and I still gotta churn and it's 4 o'clock now. Hope to see you soon.

Beulah Mae

Chapter 4

Luck's Farm

In 1947, Mama and Daddy moved from Flannigan's Farm in Radford to Richmond, Virginia. Harless was six years old, I was five, Doris was four and Nancy was two. They moved onto a farm owned by C. Merle Luck of Luck Quarries. Daddy would run the farm for Mr. Luck. The land the farm was located on was sizeable, around 300 acres, and was named Bologna Arsenal. It was used by the South during the Civil War as a stronghold against the Yankees as well as being an arsenal where the cannon shot was made and stored. There was the large main house the Lucks lived in, white frame with columns that made it look like a castle to me, with several smaller storage sheds close by the main house also painted white. A wooden fence bordered the road leading into Bologna Arsenal, three rows of white boards – a half mile of it -- and the fence went all the way up the road to the farm house, which was where we lived. The house we lived in was provided for the farm manager and was away from the main house, about a quarter of a mile away, across a wide pasture with a dirt road leading to the farm house and barns. There was one huge barn and cows and pigs and chickens and a prize bull. Daddy took care of the farm animals and planted corn and alfalfa.

While we were living on Luck's farm was the first instance of Daddy running around on Mama. In the late 1940s, it was called running around. Today it's called being unfaithful. I think running around covers it better. His running around was always in conjunction with his drinking too much. As we grew into adults, we would begin to realize how much of an effect the drinking would have on all of us.

In spite of this major flaw, Daddy loved us kids, even though he never knew how to show it, and was fiercely protective of us. As we grew up and learned to read and brought stories of science home to tell him, he was constantly amazed at how smart we were and how we were becoming educated. He could not read or write so his first and last goal in life was for us to get an education.

When I was in second grade, there was a boy in my class who stole my milk money every day. Milk cost a nickel and Mama wrapped my nickel up in the corner of a handkerchief and tied a knot in it so I wouldn't lose it. I left the handkerchief in my desk under the drop leaf during recess. When it came lunchtime, I would get my handkerchief out and the nickel would be gone. I had an idea who was taking it. There was a boy in my class who was dirty and a bully and I thought it was him. After my nickel got stolen two or three times, Daddy figured out a way to catch him. He took his pocket knife and notched my nickel around the edge one morning to identify it as mine, and Mama tied the notched nickel up in my handkerchief, like usual. It was stolen again that day. After school that day, Harless asked the boy to show him what was in his pockets and the dumb kid pulled out everything in his pockets and there was my notched nickel. Harless beat the devil out of him and he didn't steal my nickels any more.

Daddy had a big white-faced Hereford bull in the pasture next to the farm house. The bull's name was Bill. He was the first bull Daddy had ever owned and he had him gentled like a pet. Daddy had babied him, feeding him treats until he was tame. Us kids would walk up to him and pet him like a large dog. One Sunday, Mama dressed all of us girls in identical pinafore dresses she had made on her sewing machine. Daddy put us all up on the back of the bull, one behind the other, and Mama took our picture. When we straddled the bull, he was so broad across the back that our legs stuck straight out. I remember feeling the hairs on his back scratch the undersides of my legs.

Sometimes we would ride on the tractor with Daddy, standing beside him holding on to the back of the tractor seat. The tractor was started by moving a lever on the side of the steering wheel from the down position forward to the up position. I had watched him start the tractor using this lever. One day Daddy and Harless were inside the barn and had left the tractor parked idling in the road beside the barn. Mama was in the house, washing dishes in the kitchen sink. Over the sink was a window looking out to the barn. She watched as I climbed up on the seat and commenced to push the lever forward, the way I had seen Daddy do.

The tractor jerked into life and started off down the road

beside the barn. When the wheel hit the edge of the road, the tractor changed direction and it went off down the middle of the pasture, away from the barn and away from the house. There was a depression in the middle of the pasture, sort of like a sink hole, maybe at one time it was a watering hole, where the grass had grown back and the pasture sloped downward toward the hole. The tractor was headed toward that hole.

Mama saw what was happening from the kitchen window and raced out of the house. At this time she weighed over 200 and didn't move too fast but she ran across the yard and started over the white board fence that separated the house from the pasture. She made it over the fence, but when she got to the top of the fence, she misplaced her foot on the top board and fell in a heap by the fence. The tractor reached the gully and stalled out at the bottom of the gully. Daddy and Harless had heard the commotion by this time and ran to the tractor and got me off, unharmed. Mama was still sitting in a heap by the fence. She couldn't say a thing she was crying so hard.

We didn't get taken to the doctors much and only if it was a real emergency. Once I ate some honey that must have had a bee stinger in it because I swelled up like a balloon and had to be taken to the emergency room. Doris got mastoidas in her ear and had to be taken to the doctor but it was too late and she lost the hearing in that ear.

Harless taught Mama to drive our car when he was about seven. They drove around the barn and around the pastures and up and down the dirt road. He was already practiced at driving tractors and could drive our car, a Buick. Mama wanted to learn how to drive and Harless taught her on days when

Daddy was out in the field, away from the house and out of sight. The fact that Mama was learning to drive was kept from Daddy.

Harless said one day they were practicing and she was backing up and not watching where the front end of the car was going and hit the side of the barn with the right front fender. It must have been on a Saturday night because after Daddy came in from work, we were supposed to go get groceries. Mama was scared to death that Daddy was going to fuss and cuss and raise sand and he would have. She said Harless, when we get ready to go get groceries, you get out there ahead of everybody and stand in front of the fender so your Daddy can't see it. Harless went out and when Daddy came out, Daddy said Boy get in the car. Harless said I'll be there in a minute. Daddy got to fussing. Made Harless get in the car. Then Daddy saw the fender and raised the devil, just like Mama knew he would. Mama continued to learn to drive, though, despite Daddy's temper.

One time Daddy had some trash and garbage he had picked up from the Luck's house, was probably going to feed it to the hogs, and on the top of this trash was a big bag of Fritos. Harless and I were riding in the back of the truck to keep the trash under control and we got into those Fritos. We had never had Fritos before and I can remember the thrill of the taste of them to this day. I don't think Mama or Daddy ever knew that we ate out of the garbage.

Mr. Luck had some blackberry bushes and he would pay Harless by the quart to pick them in the summertime. The bushes went along the fence on the way to the Luck's house. One day Harless didn't want to pick blackberries, you would normally pick five or six quarts, and he went home and Mama said How many quarts did you pick? Harless said One. She said You didn't do a good job, go back and do it again. So he had to go back and pick the blackberries again. She knew by the number of quarts that he didn't do a good job of picking the berries. Harless got maybe a quarter for each quart of blackberries.

I got my first bicycle one Christmas while we lived on Luck's farm. It was behind the couch with a coat over it. The song "I saw Mommy Kissing Santa Claus" came out that year.

We lived on Luck's farm about four years until Daddy had a disagreement with Mr. Luck over the sale of our pigs. Mr. Luck had told Daddy that each of the children could have a pig from one of the litters and we named the pigs and fed them and took care of them, but when they were taken to market, Mr. Luck denied giving us the pigs and kept the money. There was nothing that Daddy hated more than somebody going back on their word. So he quit and we moved back to Radford just after I finished the second grade in 1950.

Chapter 5

On the Wright Farm

In 1951 Grandma Wright died of a stroke, leaving Grandpa Wright living alone in their farmhouse in Christiansburg, Virginia, about ten miles north of Radford. We had been living in Radford since moving off of Luck's Farm the year before. Grandpa and Grandma Wright lived in a house that was up a holler, built on a hill with a dirt road leading up to it. At the bottom of the hill was the milking barn, and you passed the garden, chicken house, pigpen, and horse/cow barn off to the right on your way up the hill to the house. Another chicken house, a smoke house and the johnnyhouse were out back on the other side of the main house.

Grandma Wright's funeral took place in their house. The casket was in the front room and everyone stood around in the front room, the kids standing out of the way in the hall with strict instructions from Mama to keep quiet. There had never been a funeral in our family up to that point. I remember everyone standing around quietly and Daddy's chin quivering and tears in his eyes.

Harless remembered that one time before Grandma Wright died, Mama and Daddy took him and left him on the farm with Grandma and Grandpa in Christiansburg. Every now and then, Harless would just go stay with them for a while. Grandpa Wright was up in the field behind the farmhouse using the combine on the buckwheat. They raised buckwheat for the bees. The bees took honey out of the buckwheat when it flowered and they took the buckwheat to the mill after it matured and had it ground into buckwheat flour.

Harless took off to find Grandpa, going out by the wood pile, through the gate, up in that field out behind the house and out into the field where Grandpa Wright was driving the horses, pulling the combine. Grandpa Wright was facing the other way and didn't know Harless was anywhere around. The combine was cutting the buckwheat and tying it in bundles and throwing it on the ground. Back then, the equipment didn't have all the safety features they have now. The chains were not even protected. Grandpa Wright was working the team, watching what he was doing and Harless went up behind the combine and jumped on the back of it to ride it. When he jumped on, he stuck his foot in a chain and it caught his shoe, ran it through a cog, and Harless fell off. He had tennis shoes on and after he fell off, he looked and the front of his tennis shoe was gone. So was the toenail of his big toe. Grandpa Wright kept on going because he didn't even know Harless was there. Harless went back to the house and told Grandma Wright about it. He was sitting on the back porch and she came out and was going to doctor his foot. A big old rooster was in the yard, just walking around in the yard, and he came up to the porch where Harless was sitting and pecked him on that raw place, which was bleeding, where his toenail used to be. Grandma Wright laughed at what the rooster had done. After she laughed, she doctored his toenail.

After Grandma's funeral, it was decided that we would move in with Grandpa Wright on the farm so Daddy could help him out on the farm and we could take care of Grandpa. There was 156 acres of hilly, rocky land, and a house with no running water or bathroom and it was about a mile and a half off the main road.

Harless remembered that every night Grandpa Wright had to have a certain bowl with cornbread and milk. Mama would make a pan of cornbread and he would fill the bowl with cornbread, fresh milk from the cows, and he would eat one bowl of cornbread and milk with a certain spoon, he had a certain spoon, and when he got through eating, he left the table, walked to the back door and picked up his banjo off the back of the door where he had it hanging by a strip of red satin ribbon. He would walk on out to the front porch, sit down in a rocking chair and pick his banjo for a while, then go to bed. That was his ritual. Every night, cornbread and milk and banjo and bed.

Grandpa Wright played the old timey flailing style of picking, which used more chords and less picking of individual strings. He played his banjo on the front porch while we shelled pinto beans. Everybody called them October beans because they were gathered in the fall. Rows and rows of October beans were planted every year and everyone in the family had to work in the garden to pick them. When the beans had filled out and were ready to be picked, we would pull up the whole bean plant and carry the plants to the front porch. Huge mounds of bean plants were piled on the porch and Grandpa would play while we shelled out the beans. Mama canned the beans and there was always a bowl of October beans on the supper table, sometimes with homemade sausage cooked in them.

Grandpa Wright and Daddy kept twenty-five or thirty beehives on a rock cliff, out away from the house. They had placed the beehives on the cliff so the cows wouldn't get mixed up with the hives. Daddy wore a veil and used a smoke gun to get the honey out of the hives. Grandpa Wright would take Harless and go out and hunt wild bees.

Harless remembered that Grandpa Wright would get a bottle of what he called sweet annison (it was probably anise and Grandpa mispronounced it like it had been mispronounced for a long time by country people) *and he would take Harless and go into the woods. Grandpa Wright would take a leaf and he'd put a drop of that sweet annison on a leaf and put it on a stump. Grandpa Wright didn't have any teeth, and he would take a little bit of that stuff and put it in his mouth and mist it in the air. Then he and Harless would sit there and watch and it wouldn't be long before the bees would come to it. The bees could smell it because it was sweet. The bees would find it and eat it and they would circle up, go up in the air and circle around a couple of times and then go right straight to the tree where they were making their hive and their honey. Then Grandpa Wright would take the leaf up and move it to another stump, follow the bee in the direction he was going, and put it down again. And the bees would come back again. And eventually they would find the bee tree. Once they found the bee tree, Grandpa Wright would cut the tree down and get the honey and sometimes he could take and cut a block of the tree out and take that back to the farmhouse and that would be the hive, he would save the whole hive that way and that would increase his bee population.*

When the bees would swarm in the summertime, sometimes they would light on a tree or a bush that was low to the ground. Daddy would take a dish pan and shake the bees into the dishpan and take the dishpan of bees over and gently pour it in front of a hive. *Harless told me that what he was doing was shaking off the queen because the queen would fly just a short distance from the hive, and she would light and all the other bees would cluster around her and make the bee swarm. There would be half a bushel of bees around her. When they were in this swarm stage, Daddy would shake them into the dishpan and when he poured them out in front of the empty new hive, an empty one that he would have ready, the queen would crawl into the new beehive and all the other bees would follow her.* If it was up in a tree, he would have to shoot it down, with a rifle, make the limb fall and he would have the hive ready and put them into the hive.

Chapter 6

Grandpa Wright's Banjo

$\mathcal{O}$n weekends, Grandpa Wright would go to the local beer joints where they would be playing Bluegrass music, walking by himself down the dirt road from the farmhouse to the main road. He would walk, carrying his banjo with the strap across his back. He liked to play his banjo in a beer joint about two miles from the farmhouse where we lived. He would walk there on Saturday night after the milking was done and he would play for beers and then walk home. About a year after we moved in with him, we kids were asleep in the bedrooms upstairs when Daddy came to tell us that Grandpa Wright was dead. He was walking back from the beer joint in the middle of the night and had been hit by a car while walking along the side of the road, or he was probably wandering in the road from too many beers.

Mama and Daddy bought the farm after Grandpa died. The farm was sold at auction because there were twelve children, so each child would realize part of the farm. Three of Daddy's brothers were in the audience to make the price of the farm go way up so they would get more money for their share or maybe it was just to spite Daddy. Daddy fooled them and got another man to bid for him and the farm was auctioned for a reasonable price, and the brothers were all mad as hell. Daddy didn't have anything to do with those brothers for the rest of his life.

Daddy continued to farm the land and he did a good job making that rocky, hilly land produce. It's an old cliché to say he worked from sun up 'til sundown, but he did, and so did we. Daddy planted alfalfa and about twenty acres of corn. The corn was for making silage for the cows. Silage is defined in Webster's dictionary as green fodder preserved in a silo. Silage was made from the ripened stalks of corn in late summer. When the corn was ripe, we had to cut it down with a machete and grind it up for silage. The full grown corn rows were three feet over my head and walking down the corn row was like being under a shade tree. We had dairy cows and Daddy sold the milk and cream. We always had plenty of fresh milk in crocks in the refrigerator, the surface of the milk yellow where an inch of cream had risen to the top. The cream was churned into butter in a tall wooden churn with a long handle. Churning was one of my chores.

Mama would skim the cream off the top of the crocks of milk and put it in the churn. The churn was a large wooden bucket, in the shape of an A, about three feet tall, bigger around at the bottom than it was on the top, and it had a lid that fit down onto the top with a hole in the lid big enough for the churn handle to fit into. The churn handle was just a straight piece of wood, like a broom handle, and it fit down into the churn through the hole in the lid. The end of the churn handle that went into the churn had a hexagonal plate affixed to the end of the churn handle that was also wooden.

After the cream went in and the churn handle was put in the churn and the lid went down over the handle, the job of churning was simple. Grab the churn handle with both hands and raise it straight up in the air until it cleared the cream and then plunge it back down again into the cream. By repeating this raising and plunging action, the cream was transformed into butter. I would sit with the churn between my legs and pull the churn handle up and down, over and over and over. The closer the cream got to being butter, the harder it was to raise the handle. The big floor radio was on the wall next to the dinner table and I used to sit at the end of the table and churn butter on Saturday mornings and listen to Buster Brown on the radio. *I'm Buster Brown, I live in a shoe. My dog's name is Tide. He lives there too. Plunk your magic plunker, froggie.* You can say that phrase to anyone born between 1940 and 1950 and they will immediately remember it as Buster Brown on the radio.

The radio was our only form of entertainment. The family favorite was Grand Old Opera (always pronounced Grand Ole Opry) on Saturday night, and the antics of Jack Benny and Rochester. Red Skelton doing Heathcliff. Daddy pounded his knee and laughed.

Mama cooked on the wood stove and it provided the heat for the whole downstairs of the farmhouse. Upstairs where we slept was freezing cold in the winter but the beds were weighted down with homemade quilts, so heavy you could barely move under them.

Harless and I had to milk the cows in the morning before

we went to school, but first we had to go up on the side of the mountain and drive the cows down off the hill where they had been sleeping and resting during the night. The cows made paths through the woods up the hill and they followed these same paths every time they went up or down the hill, one cow behind the other. Mama would put our boots in the oven of the wood stove to warm them up. We didn't wear any gloves but your hands would get warm as soon as the milking got started and you could get your hands under the warm udders of the cows.

We herded the cows into the milking barn, about seven cows at a time. There were about twenty cows, total. Most of the milking was done by Harless and me because Doris and Nancy were still too little. *Once we had an old red cow and she balked at going into the barn. Harless got tired of waiting around for her to decide to go into the barn and he picked up a rock and threw it at her and it hit her right behind her front leg. She dropped in her tracks like she had been shot. It scared Harless to death because he thought he had killed the cow. And Daddy would have killed him if he had. But, after a while, she came around and got back up and went on into the barn.*

There were stanchions in a row in the barn with places for the cows to put their heads in the stanchions. On the other side of the stanchions was a long trough filled with silage and the cows would go stick their heads into the stanchions to eat the silage and we would close the stanchion around their head so they couldn't back out. They would then be held in place and we could sit down beside each cow with a milking stool and a bucket and milk her. I remember the distinctive sour smell of the silage, which I liked, as it came out of the shoot of the silo, inside the barn, and it would be steaming from where it was "working" in the silo. We would milk the cows by hand, and strain the milk into big galvanized steel milk cans that held about twenty gallons of milk. We used a special strainer big enough to fit the mouth of the milk can, put a filter pad in the bottom of the strainer and poured the milk through the strainer into the milk can.

Sometimes the cows would change positions while they were standing there eating, moving their hind ends right or left, taking the weight off one or the other foot. If you weren't paying attention, just milking away trying to get the chore done, the cow would step on your feet or step in your bucket and spill all the milk on the floor. Sometimes their udders would be cracked and you had to put ointment on them or would be caked with mud and you had to clean them off before you could milk. The cows did not like any of this and would move around as much as they could inside the stanchion to get away from you and make the job hard for a kid to handle. This was one of the many chores that we grew up doing, not realizing at the time how much this was building our character. (As I am writing this book, the term "character building" in present-day terms is relayed by parents to teenagers to describe anything that requires hard work.)

I had a cow of my own named Shorty. She was brownish red all over and short, small for a cow and she had only three udders, but they were huge. You had to take two hands to hold one of her udders. She had big hooves that would completely cover one of my feet. While I was milking her, she would swat the flies with her tail and her tail would come around and smack you right upside your face. I bought her with my own money when I was about ten. Daddy would give each of us a calf and when the calf was sold off, would give us the money but we always had to buy a cow with the money. I paid $60 for her.

Chapter 7

Carrying Water

We didn't have indoor plumbing and Mama had to carry water up the hill from the springhouse to cook, clean, wash clothes and bathe us. We only had one bath a week, in a big galvanized tub in the middle of the kitchen. Mama had to carry the water from the springhouse and heat it on the wood stove. All of us kids bathed, one after the other, in the same water, warmed up with a fresh pan of hot water in between kids. The springhouse was just a shed, built to straddle the natural spring that came out of the rocks and it had a cement trough built through the middle of the shed so that you could sit things in the cold water to keep them cold, like crocks of milk and butter. *Harless said he would come in after baling hay and would bend down and bury his whole face in the cold water.* The springhouse was DOWN the hill from the house so that Mama had to carry the full buckets of water UP the hill. We had to carry water too and the buckets were heavy and hurt your hands so that you had to set the buckets down every few feet to rest your hands. We never had indoor plumbing or a bathroom, but Daddy finally put pipes in to run water into the kitchen.

We kept chickens for eggs and for Sunday dinner. There was a woodpile out behind the house. A big stump beside the woodpile was used as a chopping block where we cut up wood and kindling and a hatchet was always left sticking in the stump. Mama would get behind a chicken and grab its legs and carry it, head down, out to the stump. She would swing the chicken up on the chopping block, swing the hatchet and cut the chicken's head off and toss the chicken over behind the woodpile, where it would flop around until it died. Then she would take the chicken and dip it in a bucket of scalding water and pick off all of the feathers. She made fried chicken with gravy, mashed potatoes, corn on the cob, green beans, and biscuits from scratch for Sunday dinner and blackberry cobbler for dessert. There was always apple butter and honey from Grandpa Wright's hives to put on hot biscuits.

Mama occasionally bought magazines named *Modern Romance* and *True Confessions*, along with the *Saturday Evening Post*. I wasn't allowed to read the romance magazines because there were stories in there of wayward girls. I would take them and a salt shaker and climb up in the apple tree behind the house and read while I ate green apples with salt. She caught me once up in the tree reading the forbidden magazines and stood at the bottom of the tree and ordered me to come down and get her a switch. I told her many years later that those books taught me a valuable lesson. After reading those heartbreaking stories about those young girls who got into trouble for going "all the way" with boys, I wasn't about to let such a thing happen to me. And so, in the way of parenting since the beginning of time, what she thought would give me the wrong ideas gave me just the opposite.

In the fall, Mama and Daddy made apple butter in a big copper cauldron out in the yard on the side of the house. Mama's clothesline was over there in the same area. She hung up clothes with wooden clothespins that had no metal springs. We used Grandpa Wright's apple peeler that was attached to the edge of the table to peel all of the apples that went into the apple butter. By placing one apple at a time on it and cranking the handle, the apple would turn and a blade would be moved up close to the apple to peel it. The apples would have to be cored by hand and thrown into the cauldron. They would make a big fire under the cauldron and it would be kept going all day and the apples would cook up into a mush. Somebody had to keep stirring the apples all of the time with a wooden ladle about five feet long, made in the L shape of a boat rudder. They would stand on the side of the kettle with that wooden ladle and move around and around the fire stirring the apples. The pot would hold thirty or forty gallons. *Harless said that Grandpa Wright would put a penny in the bottom of the kettle to keep the apples from sticking.* When the apples cooked to a mush, the cinnamon and other spices would go in, and then it would be put into jars. They used an old metal dipper to get it into the cans. After the day's batch was done, we would have fresh apple butter on biscuits with churned butter.

Daddy would kill squirrels with his 22 rifle and skin them and Mama would fry them for dinner and make squirrel gravy. There was a handmade wooden chest on the porch that held the cornmeal and flour. It was about three feet deep and divided down the middle. Bulk flour was kept on one side and cornmeal on the other. Mama made fresh bread for almost every meal, cornbread or biscuits. There was an extra stove stored on the porch too, and one Christmas, Mama hid our presents in the oven of the stove. She had to find extra special hiding places for our presents because Harless would make it his goal to find our Christmas presents every year.

We finally got an electric washing machine and that was put out on the screened porch too. It had legs with roller wheels and a ringer press mounted on top. Mama had to carry water from the springhouse to put in the washing machine. After the clothes had been put through the washing cycle, you turned on the ringer press and fed the wet clothes through the press to get the water out. Then fill the tub with water again for rinsing and repeat the process of putting the clothes through the ringer at the end of the rinse cycle so you could hang the clothes on the line. I got my arm caught in the ringer press one time when I was feeding clothes through the ringer. My arm was in the ringer up past my elbow. I was nine or ten at the time. Mama ran out on the porch when I started hollering and calmly turned the crank off and wound my arm back out of the ringer press. I can't imagine how I got it caught in there to begin with. Probably wanted to see what would happen if I fed my arm into it. In the wintertime, the clothes would be so stiff when you took them off the clothesline, you could stand a pair of overalls up in the floor and they would stand there by themselves.

We had chickens and ducks and a rooster with sharp claws who would lie in wait for us to come near the henhouse to gather eggs so that he could charge us, squawking to high heaven with his feathers all puffed up and mean looking. Nancy was especially scared of the rooster and would have to throw things at him to get him away from the henhouse long enough to gather the eggs. It was an uneven fight because Nancy was only about six or seven.

Mama always wore aprons when she was cooking or canning, most of them handed down from Big Granny and even a couple were handed down from Grandma Wright. They were all made by hand, sewn on a Singer, from hardy cotton, with pockets. If not pockets, they had three sections in front like you would find in a carpenter's apron. They were made with a bib in the front to protect the front of your blouse or dress. The bib was kept in place with a strap sewn in that went over your head. Made for adults, these aprons were comical when we kids put them on to help Mama in the kitchen. They had been washed so much they were as soft as velvet and had that terrific odor of being ironed. Mama used her apron as a potholder for removing hot pans from the stove or oven. Or for carrying eggs, little chicks, vegetables from the garden, apples off of trees, and kindling from the woodpile. Or for wiping kids' sweaty faces, dusting furniture, holding October beans during the shelling, and carrying out the hulls of beans shelled. There were probably a lot of germs on her apron, but I don't think I ever caught anything from an apron.

Chapter 8

BBs, Boyfriends and Saplings

Mama fried pork tenderloin on the stove in the morning to make us sandwiches to go in our school lunch. All the other kids had bologna and cheese sandwiches and I thought we were poor because we had to take fried tenderloin sandwiches in our lunch.

We went to the county fair every year and I remember Daddy would gamble away a lot of money at those games where you throw rings and hit a coke bottle, or throw a dime to hit a plate. He would stay there and gamble away a lot of money if Mama didn't pull him away. At that time people didn't know how crooked the games were.

I remember going to the fair once and there was a friend of mine from school at the fair with her mother. They were standing next to a French fry stand. As kids, we never had any money and never got treats like French fries. My friend and her mother bought some French fries in a cone, a paper cone and put vinegar on them and I don't recall ever having French fries before that time, and especially French fries with vinegar on them and I thought they were so good. I wanted the whole thing to myself. It stands out because I thought they were so rich because they could just buy French fries like it was an everyday thing.

While we were living on the farm, I had my first boyfriend, Jimmy McGee. I was twelve or thirteen. For Christmas he gave me this tiny little bottle of dime-store perfume, probably cost a quarter, but it was special. It was really loud-smelling and I didn't ever use it and I think I finally threw it away when I was a teenager.

Harless shot me in the finger with his BB gun while we were out on the front porch of the farmhouse. I had laid my candy bar on the railing of the porch while we were out there shelling October beans. I went to pick it up and Harless said Don't touch that candy or I'll shoot it off the porch. As I grabbed for my candy bar, he shot the BB and it hit me in the finger. Mama whipped him good. I still have the scar. Harless grins when I remind him of his meanness.

One of our chores was for Harless and me to go up on the hill behind the milk barn and cut the bark off the locust saplings. You would take a knife and cut a ring around the top and strip the bark away from the tree and the tree would die. This was the easiest way to get rid of sapling trees before they got too big. We were walking back to the house in the cow path after one of these days of stripping saplings, and suddenly something spooked the two work horses that were grazing on the side of the hill where we were working. The horses came thundering down the hill in the same cow path but behind us and were bearing down on us. Harless jumped to the side of the path, up the hill, out of the way of the stampeding horses and he was yelling at me to do the same. I was scared to death and I couldn't figure out what he wanted me to do. I was running as fast as I could and I could hear those big horse's hooves pounding behind me and Harless kept yelling and finally it got through to me what he wanted me to do and I jumped up the side of the hill off the path. Just when I did that, the horses thundered by and I sat down on the side of the path and cried and cried because I was so scared. I don't know if the horses would have run me down or not but I was sure of it at the time. Harless said You're okay, you're okay.

In the summer when the blackberries got ripe, Mama would take us kids and several big buckets and we would go up on the hill behind the milk barn to pick blackberries. We would spend several hours picking blackberries and our fingers and lips were blue from the berry juice. It seemed like gallons and gallons of blackberries and we would carry the full buckets home down the hill. Sometimes we would empty our milk buckets into a big galvanized tub and carry the tub between us down the hill to the house. Mama would can them for blackberry pies in the winter and make blackberry jam to put on biscuits with a little lake of butter.

There was a mulberry tree along one of the fences by the house and I remember those long seedpods from the mulberry tree and we tried unsuccessfully to smoke them. They wouldn't stay lit.

Nancy got polio the summer she was about seven while we were living on the Wright farm. Mama and Daddy had gone to town to get groceries and left us kids there at the house. We were playing out in the yard when Harless realized something was wrong. *Nancy was just sort of sprawled out on the grass sleeping and not moving. When Mama came home and tried to get her up, they realized something was awfully wrong and rushed her to the hospital. The doctors said she had polio and had probably gotten it from playing in the creek.* She would have to be given very hot baths so her legs wouldn't be affected and Mama had to carry water from the springhouse and heat it on the stove and give her several hot baths a day and Nancy would scream when Mama put her in the water but the doctors said do it and Mama listened to the doctors and did it. Mama prayed and Nancy got over the polio and wasn't paralyzed. Nancy chewed on Harless' teddy bear which didn't have any eyes to get through the pain.

After Daddy put in the pipes for water to come into the kitchen, Mama didn't have to haul water from the springhouse to wash dishes but she still had to heat it on the stove. She used a box of Tide for washing clothes and the dishes. Once she left me in the kitchen to wash the dishes and she put the Tide in the water and went off to do something else. I splashed the water around and found out the more you splashed, the more bubbles it made and then I decided to add more Tide to make more bubbles and when Mama came back I had bubbles all over the kitchen sink and on the floor. Of course Mama gave me a lecture about being wasteful and how much things cost and here I was playing in it and I felt so bad I never ever forgot that lesson. I remembered that instance every time I used Tide for a long, long time. I wonder if the Tide people would like to know that.

Chapter 9

Feed Sacks and Home Perms

During the winter, if the corn ran out, Daddy would have to buy pig feed in fifty-pound sacks from the feed store. It was called pig mash. It was ground up corn and had the consistency of flour. The pig mash came in cotton sacks that had pretty flowers printed on them and after the pig mash was used up, Mama washed the sacks and cut them up and made dresses for us girls from the feed sacks. She would sew borders of bric-a-brac on the necks and sleeves.

Daddy's sister Dorothy, who was hilarious and fun to be around, would come to the farmhouse and give us home permanents. That was when Daddy started calling me possum because after these home permanents, my hair stuck out all over.

Daddy bought a small jeep with a rag top and seats in the back big enough for two children. He would take the four of us in the jeep down the dirt road about a mile to meet the school bus at the main road. When the school bus let us out in the afternoon, we walked home. We had a mixed-breed Collie and sometimes he would meet us halfway home. After school my favorite snack was saltine crackers in a bowl of milk. That was also one of Daddy's favorite things to eat, even when he was eighty-nine years old and living by himself after Mama died, a bowl of saltine crackers and milk. We rarely had store-bought candy, but Mama made peanut butter and chocolate candy on the stove by melting butter and sugar in a frying pan and cooking it until it thickened and she could pour it out to cool on sheets of waxed paper.

During the summers when we were out of school, Harless and I helped Daddy with the farm work and Doris and Nancy helped Mama in the house. Harless and I milked cows, baled hay, cut and stacked corn, made silage, and rounded up the cows. Everybody worked in the garden and fed the chickens and ducks and pigs and gathered eggs. On Saturday night after working all day every day that week, our treat would be to go to the drive-in movies. Mama's brother, Uncle Bud, worked the ticket office at the theater and most of the time would wave us on in for free. Daddy got such a kick out of getting in free. *Ma and Pa Kettle* movies would be playing, or *Laurel and Hardy* and Daddy would laugh so loud the people in the cars around us would stare or laugh at him. We didn't have enough money to go to the snack bar. The best part was the *Woody Woodpecker* cartoon before the movie started. Sometimes we kids would sit on the hood of the car to watch the movie. There was a playground with swings down in front of the cars at the foot of the big movie screen and we were sometimes allowed to go down there to play. It was a treat to play with the other children in the semi-darkness with only the light from the movie playing over our heads.

We had two work horses, their names were Molly and Dan, for plowing and mowing hay. *Harless was big enough to plow by himself with Molly. He plowed corn with a three-point cultivator, where you had to go down each row twice, once on each side. Molly was so used to plowing that he didn't have to say anything to her, she knew what to do. They would get to the end of the row and all he had to do was swing the plow out of the way and she would come back around and start off down the row at the right place. She would take her time, she had big feet, and she would step on a few hills of corn now and then. At dinnertime, which was the noonday meal, Harless would come in, leave the harness on her, and take her down to the spring where the water came out of the spring house. Harless was always barefooted and every day Molly would step on his feet and he would be pushing on that big horse trying to get her off his foot. Then he would take her to the barn and give her three or four ears of corn, she had lunch while he had lunch, and then he would go back and get her, put the bridle on her and go back and plow some more. He would sometimes plow with both horses, turning the sod, then you would have to take a disc and break up the sod. Daddy would harness the horses, put Harless on one of the horses, and give him the reins of the other, the plows were already in the field. They were good work horses and were accustomed to working in the rocky soil. When he hit a rock they would stop. And he would drag the plow around the rock and they'd start again. The horses were so big he couldn't get on from the ground, so he would put the horses next to the fence and climb up the fence to get on. Harless was about ten years old.*

The Sweeney family on the next farm was one of the few

families to have a television. It was a floor model RCA. There were only floor models then, in a wooden cabinet and the screen was about nine inches across. During the summer on Wednesday nights we would go over to the Sweeney's house to watch television, *I love Lucy* and *What's My Line*. The picture was so snowy you could hardly see it but we thought it was great. Willard Sweeney and his wife couldn't have children, but they kept a boy whose name was Danny who had features like an American Indian, handsome, dark complexioned, big brown eyes and dark black hair. He was a few years older than me. I had a crush on him. His parents lived in the neighborhood but they were trashy, so the Sweeneys took him in. Harless, who was about twelve years old, would sometimes drive us over to the Sweeneys in the jeep. It wasn't dangerous or anything because at the end of our dirt lane where the hard surface road started there wasn't any traffic and it wasn't that far.

I vividly remember another occasion involving good-looking Danny, when I was about twelve. Daddy sometimes made homebrew, which is homemade beer, and we would have picnics at this particularly pretty spot down by the creek about a half a mile from the house. My Uncle Fred and Aunt Edith would be invited and they would bring along some more friends and my Uncle Bud would bring a date. Uncle Fred and Uncle Bud were the only Sutphins who had ever had anything alcoholic to drink and they loved Daddy's homebrew. We never told Big Granny or Granddaddy or the other Sutphin sisters that homebrew was served at these picnics.

The Sweeneys were also invited and Danny came with them. Mama had made me a new dress which I couldn't wait to show off to the company and I was so very excited about seeing Danny at the party. There were several children at the party and we chased each other and played and were having a great time until Mama decided I was going to get my new dress dirty so she took it off of me, lifted it right over my head. I had a slip on underneath, but it was the most horrendous, embarrassing thing Mama had ever done, taking my dress off right there in front of everybody. She was completely oblivious to my embarrassment so when I started crying and got in the road and walked home, she couldn't figure out what was wrong with me. She apologized later but I was never able to be around Danny again.

Other memories on the farm involved the making of silage. Harless and I would go with Daddy to the cornfield and cut off the corn stalk at the base of the stalk with a machete and lay the stalk down on the ground beside the corn row. Daddy would drive the wagon pulled by the horses along the row and we would throw the corn stalks onto the wagon. *Harless said it was a four-wheeled, iron-wheeled wagon, no sides on the wagon so you would have to throw it crossways of the wagon or it would slide off the back. After the wagon was loaded down with corn, Daddy would drive the wagon out of the bumpy cornfield and down the rocky dirt road to get it back to the barn. The corn was so slick it would slide off anyway and we would have to reload it. It was almost impossible to get the road level because the land was so rocky. The horses were good at pulling the wagon, but once they put their weight into the harness, they couldn't slow down and if the corn started to slide, a lot of it would slide off before we could stop the horses. Hot, hard work.* Big stalks of corn and it would be green and the blades would cut your arm. When we got the corn back to the silo, which was right beside the barn, we fed the corn an armload at a time onto a conveyor that moved the corn stalks along into a grinder. The grinder was like a big fan with huge blades and was as big around as the wheel of the tractor.

Daddy had the jeep hooked up to a motor that ran the conveyor. The ground corn stalks were fed into the silo through a long chute. Harless and I had to stand inside the silo and stomp down the silage as it came out of the chute so it wouldn't clog up at the mouth of the chute. Sometimes it would get clogged up and it would stop up the chute and Daddy would fuss at us because we couldn't keep up. It was hot and stinky in the silo and I can still recall the smell of it. The concrete silo was about eight stories high with a small wooden side door at each floor for entry/exit out onto a ladder affixed to the side of the silo. As the silo filled up, we would emerge after each wagonload of corn was ground up through the side door with silage in our hair, in our noses and ears, and stuck to our clothes. We had to help because Daddy couldn't afford to hire any help.

Daddy always planted more corn than he needed for silage so we could have corn for the hogs and cows and horses in the wintertime. He would leave some corn in the field until it dried on the stalk. We cut that corn and stacked it in shocks in the field. A shock was what you called it when you gathered about thirty cornstalks together, with the corn still on the stalks and tied it together with fodder twine around the middle so it stood on its own after it was tied up. There was a special tool to put fodder twine around the shock, and once it was tied up, it was left in the field. *Harless said in the wintertime, if we needed corn, you would push the shock over. Harless and Daddy would get on one side of it and push it over, and it would roll over on its side and they'd get on their knees to shuck the corn. Daddy on one side and Harless on the other and they would shuck the corn and throw it into a pile and take the fodder that was left and haul it to the cattle. Take the corn to the hogs and the horses. Some mornings it would be snowing and they would have to move the snow to get to the corn.*

You shucked the corn with a tool that you wore on your right hand. It had a metal part in the middle that was curved on the end so you could grab the corn shuck and pull it towards you to shuck the corn. Some of the corn was shucked and put into a big wooden bin that was the corn crib in the barn. Sometimes when you reached into the corn crib to take out some corn, you would surprise a mouse and you would jump two feet off the ground when it jumped out and ran away.

Chapter 10

Alfalfa

$\mathcal{D}$addy planted alfalfa to make hay to feed the cows and horses in the winter when there was no grass for them to graze. Daddy and Harless would harvest the alfalfa with a team of horses and a hay mower. *Harless said that it was hard on the horses to pull the mower because the horses had to go fast, at a trot most of the time, to keep the blade working fast enough to cut the alfalfa. It was eight or ten inches tall, thick and lush, and they would have to trot, walk real fast and you would have to stop every so often and let them catch their breath. They would be breathing hard and lathered with sweat, all of their harness straps would be lathered white with sweat. They would go around the field, start on the outside, and around and around Daddy would go, each time getting closer to the middle. When he would get down to the middle, Harless would go on the opposite side from where Daddy was cutting. Rabbits would run out and Harless would catch them because a rabbit doesn't run straight, they zig-zag and Harless would run straight and eventually would catch them. Sometimes the rabbits wouldn't get out of the way of the*

mower fast enough and the mower blade would cut them in two.
And they would come out with no legs, flopping around.

After a few days, the alfalfa would dry out and they would rake it up into piles with a horse-drawn rake, then load the piles of hay onto the wagon with a pitchfork and haul it to the barn. In the hayloft at the barn, there was a huge hook with three arms, on a pulley and it would come down and grab the hay. The pulley would be worked by attaching one end of the rope to a horse and leading the horse away from the barn. The pulley with the rope would haul it into the hayloft. There were holes cut in the floor of the loft to drop the hay down to the cows and horses. That was how we harvested the hay for a few years before Daddy got another farmer with a hay baler to come over and help us bale the hay.

We didn't have enough money for Daddy to get any help, so all of the farm work was done by him and Mama and us kids. We were forever getting cuts and bruises, but no broken bones. There were few things that we encountered that got a doctor's attention. Fevers were waited out, cuts were usually treated with merthiolate or iodine, runny noses were common and we all got croup every winter.

Once when I was sick, Mama wanted to have me in the kitchen where she could tend to me so she lined up three chairs in a row along the wall in the kitchen, next to the wood stove, and put pillows on the chairs and that was my bed. I was a little glad that I was sick because you didn't often get her undivided attention and it was warm and smelled good in the kitchen. Mama did her best to tend to us. I had a lot of fever blisters during the time we lived on the farm and Mama didn't know any better, she put merthiolate on them which burned to high heaven and made me cry harder. Sometimes she would put bacon grease on the fever blisters, which felt better than merthiolate, but it didn't do anything to heal the blisters. We didn't go to the dentist either until we moved to Richmond. We were all teenagers by that time and I recall I had thirteen cavities.

Chapter 11

Richmond

*M*ama and Daddy decided to sell the farm in Christiansburg and we moved to Richmond, Virginia, about 200 miles to the East, in 1955 into a house with a bathroom. Daddy had been offered a job in construction working for Mr. Luck (of the Luck's Farm story), so Daddy sold the farm and made a good profit and we packed up and left farm life for good.

Mama and Daddy paid $15,000 for the house in Richmond and paid all but $2,000 in cash because they had scrimped and saved and done without for many years. They signed a note for the $2000 balance, and although the note was paid off within two years, it worried both of them because they had never signed a note for anything before.

We kids cried and objected loudly when we left Wright's farm and questioned why we were moving when things were going so well on the farm. The barn was full of hay, we had gotten old enough and big enough to do most of our chores, and the rhythm of planting, harvesting, making apple butter, and tending cows we had named had given us security. It was agreeable to us, though it was hard. However, we were also becoming teenagers and being passionate at that age, were probably a lot more dramatic about moving than was necessary.

Once we got to Richmond, things settled down and we began to appreciate living off the farm. Yard work and housework were nothing compared to farm work, even though Daddy immediately planted two gardens and we were still expected to work in the garden. Shortly after we moved into the house on Ruthers Road on the South side of Richmond, we bought a television and a washing machine and we all started taking a bath much more often than once a week. We had a well for water and Daddy was the dictator of water usage, always worrying about the well running dry. He fussed at Mama because she was running water at the sink to wash vegetables and often asked why we had to take so many baths. His bath consisted of a washing off at the bathroom sink, the sink stoppered up to hold about a gallon of water.

When we moved to Richmond, Harless was fourteen, I was thirteen, Doris was twelve and Nancy was ten. The house on Ruthers Road was where we would grow into teenagers, come home from college, get married, and bring our children and grandchildren for the next forty-eight years. Doris had her own small bedroom and Nancy and I shared a large bedroom upstairs, where Harless also had his own room. We were all teenagers but we still watched *Mickey Mouse Club* after school because we had not seen that much television, especially kid shows or cartoons. We watched *Father Knows Best, American Bandstand* and *The Ed Sullivan Show* starring Ricky Nelson and Elvis. We enrolled in the high school and joined the local

Methodist Church and the Methodist Youth Fellowship. We were hicks but we had been taught manners and learned fast and were all popular with the other high school and neighborhood teenagers.

Midlothian Turnpike, about one half mile away from our house, was the closest main highway and was undeveloped with only one stoplight between our house and the shopping center, which was the first shopping center in Southside Richmond and was called Southside Plaza. It was about three miles away and was built around 1957. This was not a mall with a food court, it was a string of stores all with their separate entrances from the outside.

Nearby was Bill's Barbeque, a drive-in with carhops who delivered the barbeques and hamburgers on trays with brackets that fit on the open window of the driver's side door. On weekends we rode through the parking lot of Bill's to check out the boys and to see who was dating whom and who was parked in the back row where the lighting was dim so they could neck. Whatever was playing on the jukebox was broadcast from speakers to the outside so there was always the sound of rock and roll, boys revving their cars and girls hanging out of the car windows, embarrassing themselves hollering at the boys and not even realizing it.

By this time, to us Mama had become the one who held the family together, the one who kept us clear on the difference between right and wrong and the one who urged us to go to Sunday school and church. She didn't go herself but she made sure we had clean clothes and our crinolines were starched and our shoes polished. She vowed to give us the freedom she had been denied while she was growing up. Daddy was the one who went to work at dawn, worked hard all day, knew all there was to know about farming and planting gardens, the one who bragged about us kids to strangers and never spent a penny on anything frivolous. Mama laid down the law and disciplined us on the golden rule and the Ten Commandments, praying on her knees by her bed for Harless' safety while he was playing football at the high school (she made us girls get down on our knees and pray too).

The next five years while we were teenagers was to me the happiest time of my life. We were growing up but not grown and there was so much to discover. The girls wore bobby socks and poodle skirts and starched crinolines and the Everly Brothers sang "Wake Up Little Suzie" and Fats Domino sang "I Found My Thrill On Blueberry Hill." Harless and I played high school sports. He played football and was a shot putter on the track team. I played basketball and field hockey and played catcher on the church softball team. We had to bum rides home from school after football practice or basketball practice because we only had one car and Daddy drove it to work.

Daddy worked for Mr. Luck on a construction crew, operating a front loader and digging ditches. Mama went to work in the school cafeteria as a cook when I was in the tenth grade. The year that Harless was a senior, all of us had dates and went to the prom. All four of us lined up in the front room with our dates for pictures. There was some smoking and drinking by some of the kids in high school, but the ones who did had bad reputations. I don't recall it ever entered my mind to drink or smoke. There was heavy making out but girls did not go all the way with boys and if a girl got pregnant, she was an outcast. On the other hand, some of the boys who drank or drove fast were excused for their behavior and were still popular. There was one really handsome boy who was kind of a hood but was one of the most popular boys in school and he asked me out on a date. Harless told Mama the boy was bad news and she wouldn't let me go out with him. I was really ticked off that Harless ruined my one chance to date a celebrity. I wonder if that boy ever made anything of himself. Probably not.

Saturday mornings, Mama would be at the bottom of the stairs, hollering at us, waking us up to do cleaning or canning or washing or working in the garden. Sundays we kids usually went to church. I sang in the choir, as did my two best girlfriends, Joanie Tunstall and Diane Lowry. Joanie and I were altos and sang harmony and Diane sang soprano. Diane lived next door and Joanie lived further down Ruthers Road. Sunday nights we went to Methodist Youth Fellowship at the church and the reason was because all the boys would be there. The girls in the church who were between twelve and twenty formed a group called the Friendship Group of Girls and we went everywhere together, dressed just alike, dressed up for the boys at church, flirted with the boys at church, dated the boys at church, went steady with the boys at church and went to the proms and dances usually with the boys at church.

Diane's mother, Esther, and some of the other church mothers were our chaperones. One of the church members had a cottage on the river, near the Chesapeake Bay and they invited the Friendship Group of Girls for a weekend. God that was fun. Staying up all night, telling secrets, singing songs and sleeping on quilts on the floor. I had never done anything like it before. I learned how to pick a hard shell crab and rode in a boat on saltwater for the first time and was scared to death of drowning because I hadn't learned to swim yet. I remember Daddy was really nervous about me drowning too and didn't want me to go but Mama overrode his vote.

When I was about sixteen, Daddy started staying out late and drinking beer in the beer joints. He discovered a camaraderie in the beer joints that he had never known before and no amount of shaming him would change what became a steady habit. Mama would give him hell when he got home late at night smelling of beer, barely able to walk and certainly not able to drive.

Mama started smoking. It was a way to skip meals to help lose weight. It was a distraction that helped her get around thinking about Daddy. She needed a bit of a crutch and non-filter Chesterfields became that crutch. Cigarette smoking was popular then. Tobacco companies sponsored the majority of television programs. L.S.M.F.T. Lucky Strike Means Fine Tobacco. A few years later, filtered cigarettes were introduced to the public, the Marlboro blend was invented and Marlboro became the best selling cigarette ever produced. The main factory for Philip Morris, the maker of Marlboro cigarettes, was in Richmond and a lot of our high school classmates ended up working in the factory. Mama stuck to unfiltered Chesterfields then switched to Philip Morris Commanders, also unfiltered.

Chapter 12

College

Longwood University in Farmville, Virginia, accepted me into their freshman class in the summer of 1960. Harless had already finished his freshman year at the University of Richmond as a day student. We didn't have enough money for college, so Harless worked to make spending money while he went to school. Daddy was still working for Luck Construction so Mama suggested I go visit Mr. Luck to see if he would lend me the money for the first year's tuition, $750. He gave me a check that day and again the following year and told me not to worry about paying it back. *Harless recently told me that Mr. Luck also paid for his freshman tuition to the University, $500. I had never known that.* I expect Mr. Luck felt badly about those pigs he reneged on. I started at Longwood that fall and worked side jobs to make spending money and to pay for books.

At that time, Longwood was for girls only and primarily trained young women to be teachers. I had only been away from home overnight a couple of times and was very scared about leaving my family and living away from home. I made friends quickly though, friends that lasted a lifetime. Joyce was one of them. We were all "rushed" to join the same sorority, Alpha Chapter of Zeta Tau Alpha. The sorority was started in 1898 by a group of nine students when Longwood was known as the State Female Normal School. Belonging to the Alpha Chapter is a big deal in university fraternities. Zeta Tau Alpha embodied honor, sisterhood, integrity, and leadership. Being invited to join this group meant everything to me. I told Mama I had been invited to join, but that I wasn't going to because it cost $50 and I thought it was wasteful to spend that kind of money.

On my first weekend home from school, Mama took me in the back bedroom. The back bedroom, where the door was closed against the hearing ears of my brother and sisters, was for private talks, one-on-one, just Mama and me, usually where she gave private lectures or shared a secret that involved one of my sisters or Daddy. Still in her work clothes at the end of the day, she pressed the $50 into my hands and said, I want you to join that sorority. She didn't say another word and left me standing speechless in the bedroom. I knew she really wanted me to have it, but I cried all the way back to school. At the time she was working as a cook in the cafeteria at the high school, standing all day on a hard cement floor that killed her feet and ankles, making mashed potatoes and meatloaf for the school kids and serving it to them on their trays as they passed by in line. That $50 was almost a whole week's pay.

During my second year in college, I brought my roommate Joan home to Richmond where she visited our family doctor. He confirmed that she was pregnant. I had made an appointment with the doctor for myself. When we got there, Joan went into the examining room instead of me. Mama was with us and figured out what was going on. Joan was not married. That night my roommate called her boyfriend, the father, to tell him what she had suspected and what they had both dreaded, that she was pregnant. She took the phone and went into the little room off the living room that didn't have any heat, stretching the phone cord, so she could talk and cry in private. She had been in there about an hour when Mama went to the closet and got a quilt and carried it in there and put it around her, where she was sitting on the floor, crying and shivering. I think I loved my mother more at that moment than ever before. Joan married Abe in secret and I and her other sorority sisters helped her hide the pregnancy from the school authorities because she would have been sent home. She finished out the year, had a daughter that summer and a son the following year, and is still married to Abe. She never returned to school.

Abe's roommate was named John Watkins, whom I met and dated, also during that second year. Abe and Johnny were seniors at Virginia Tech, and Johnny and I continued to date after he graduated in 1962 and through the next summer and winter. I brought Johnny home to meet Mama and Daddy. Johnny loved Daddy instantly and Daddy, well Daddy liked him too and we all knew Daddy didn't approve of hardly any of our boyfriends. I did not return to Longwood because I had gotten a job with the Department of Defense in Richmond and discovered I could make a lot more money there than I could teaching. Johnny and I married in June 1963.

Chapter 13

Gentle

Daddy cried when he walked me down the aisle. He looked splendid in his white dinner jacket with a baby pink rose boutonniere. For once he didn't wear a hat and he didn't even ask as he knew there was no way that would be allowed. Actually, it might have been a good idea to have worn a hat to hide the large bruise on the side of his bald head where he'd gotten drunk at my rehearsal party the night before and walked into a tree by the patio. As I took his arm and started down the aisle, I could see his chin quivering and this about undid me. At the last minute as we were going into the back doors of the church, I decided the new, tight shoes I was wearing just had to go so I took them off and kicked them aside in the vestibule. When Daddy saw what I was doing, he grinned and shook his head and said Well, I never, getting married barefoot, don't that beat all. He laughed and stuck his hand in the upper left pocket of the jacket he was wearing. This was an habitual reflex motion he made often. He kept toothpicks in the pockets of his shirts, much to Mama's dismay, and reaching with his right hand into that left pocket became his signature motion.

We proceeded down the aisle, him once again tearing up and clearing his throat which was his way of gaining control of his emotions. I was the first of the four children to get married and the rehearsal the night before had been a trial for him. He didn't see what all the fuss was about and why he had to rehearse to say Her mother and I do when the preacher asked Who giveth this bride. After we got down the aisle and got to his part, he said it, not very loud, and turned halfway around to go sit with my mother, but he didn't leave right away. He just stood there sideways, lingering, his right hand again searching out that pocket. Finally he turned away.

Mama was waiting for him on the aisle in the second pew in her new blue dress and she also had on new shoes. Unlike me though, she couldn't shed hers and I knew her feet were killing her. She had bad ankles and flat arches and she had been cooking and cleaning for at least a week.

While she was getting dressed for the wedding that morning, she had grabbed up a can of what she thought was hairspray to put the final touches on her hairdo. She had had it shampooed and set the day before at the beauty parlor, a rare luxury for her. She had slept with toilet paper wound around her head to protect her hairdo and this had worked. But the can she picked up and sprayed on her hair turned out to be spray starch and this only added to her frazzled nerves and anxiety.

This was her first wedding ever and I being a college girl with modern ideas had planned and orchestrated the wedding on a very limited budget but nevertheless with class. She was anxious to leave a favorable impression on my college friends and church friends who were in the wedding and my mother and father-in-law who were from Raleigh and who were more upper crust than she was used to. I knew she was standing in the church pew on her aching feet, glad it was almost over.

All of her work was not in vain and except for the spray starch and her barefoot daughter, the wedding was beautiful and the in-laws and friends loved her and complimented her good food. My friend Joyce was my Matron of Honor; I had been her Maid of Honor two weeks before. I wrote a letter to Mama and Daddy in the living room of our house after everyone had left the rehearsal party the night before. In it I said how much I appreciated all they had done for me all my life, the sacrifices they had made, and all their hard work, including this beautiful wedding that was everything I had dreamed of. Mama kept the letter in her box of important papers and it was returned to me upon her death. I had written it when I was twenty and upon reading it again at age fifty-nine, I could feel the same gratitude that a young girl had expressed upon leaving home.

Mama also wrote letters to Johnny and me:

LETTER TO JANET (June 22, 1963: given to me to put in my suitcase when I left for my honeymoon; written in pencil on a lined tablet.)

Janet, I don't have much time, and excuse my stationery. There are a few things I would like to say, and I can write it better than say it. First of all, I want you to know how much we all love you, and every one of us will be so proud of you as you stand up there tomorrow. I know preparing for your wedding has been hectic, but I have secretly enjoyed every minute of it. I know you and Johnny didn't want a big wedding, and I want to thank you both for giving me the privilege of having one.

That's about all I wanted to say except please don't be discouraged because of mine and your Daddy's marital difficulties. I had many wonderful years, and the memories of those years I will have always. Raising you kids and planning and dreaming of just such events as is taking place right now. You have never disappointed me, of which I am very grateful. Just don't let our recent troubles discourage you. I would not swap the good years I had with your Daddy for a million dollars and if I had it to do over, I would do it again. I know he has let you down in many ways, but please try not to think of that. Instead think of the years he worked so hard for you and was the best Daddy any girl ever had for he still loves you deeply and who knows God willing maybe he will be that man again someday.

If you or Johnny ever have a problem too big to handle by yourself, please please come to me and if I can help, you know I will. It has meant an awful lot these many years having the privilege of sharing yours and the other kids problems. Well I set out to write a few lines and ended up writing a newspaper. All I want is for you both to be happy. Remember when I first met your Johnny you said get to know him and you will love him as I do and you were right. He seems like a member of the family already. If I had chosen a husband for you myself, I couldn't have done better. Wishing you both all the happiness and good luck in the world. All my love, your Mother.

LETTER TO JOHNNY (June 22, 1963; given to Johnny before we left on our honeymoon; also written in pencil on a lined tablet; money was enclosed with a note saying for honeymoon purposes only.)

Johnny, Tomorrow I will happily place in your very capable hands one of my most prized possessions, my precious daughter. The very first thing I want to say to you is I definitely do not want to be one of those mother-in-law type of people. Since your mother will be so far away, it would make me very happy if you would regard me as a substitute mother and feel free at any time to come to me with any problem you might have.

Johnny I want to give you a little hint as to what makes a woman happy. This woman in particular (Janet) she loves you dearly and I know you must love her to put up with all the wild rushing and goings on that have been taking place these last few weeks. Don't let her take for granted that you love her, if you do say so often, there's nothing a woman wouldn't do for her man if she knows he truly loves her and another thing those little things like birthdays, valentines day and such are just so much rubbish to most men but believe me Johnny they are very important. Nothing makes a woman more happy than a kiss and a happy birthday and it don't cost a cent. I know you are thinking about now, how silly I must be to write you such junk but I want you and Janet to be truly happy and know the joys I have had in many years of married life.

I am very sorry for the disinterest my husband has shown in you. I want to apologize for his many shortcomings. I wish you could have known him three years ago before he started drinking. No woman ever had a better husband and no child had a better father. I had 22 years of this, that is why I have overlooked so much in the past few years. I didn't intend to write this much what I really wanted to say was be happy and welcome to the Wright clan, and share her with us sometime. We will still love her even though she will be yours and not ours any longer. If she makes as good a wife as she has a daughter, you will not be sorry you married her. Wishing all the happiness in the world to my second son. With love your substitute mother.

LETTER TO MAMA (June 22, 2008):

Dear Mama, there are some things I want to tell you too. I got to this chapter today and didn't realize until I typed the date, the significance of the date - it was forty-five years ago that I got the letter from you on my wedding day. There was something happened the other day and I made myself a note to tell you about it, so here goes. On Mother's Day last month, Wendy bought me a Japanese Maple tree which I have wanted for a long time. I went up to Fredericksburg to her house and we went together to pick it out. It just so happened that after I had it planted, Wendy had to come here to the house and take me to one of my heart procedures. Afterward we had lunch in this really nice place and had such a good time together. When we got back to the house, we took some of your ashes and held hands and together we scattered them around the base of the tree. Wendy said Meemaw make this tree grow. So far it's growing real good. All my love, Janet.

Chapter 14

Daddy Could Not Read

$\mathcal{D}$addy could not read or write. Functionally illiterate is the proper term. I know the proper term because I have had schooling. Daddy had none. He was illiterate, and even ignorant of many things, but never stupid. In the way of people who have disabilities, he made up for it in other ways. He watched and listened. And then he proceeded to do things his own way. He had the best ability to judge people of anyone I have ever known. He could size up a person whom he had just met and be able to know within a matter of minutes if the person was honest and would be someone he liked. But he liked almost no one and sought the company of very few people during his ninety years. Yet people were drawn to him and liked him immediately.

He was a small man, only five foot seven or eight inches tall and never weighed more than 155 pounds in his life. His small, unthreatening stature and his country ways would always put a person at ease when they first met him. I suppose it had to do with psychology. Almost anyone who met him would have had more status than he. People would realize right away that here was a simple man, country, friendly, usually with old work clothes on and dirt under his fingernails. Using country words and mispronouncing the fifty cent words. And they would relax. No need to impress this old guy. And he would have them then. People would go out of their way to draw him into their crowd. Because he was unique, he never lacked for attention. Mama was good and kind, gentle, generous. But the first thing a visitor would ask is Where is Posey? Are you keeping that old man straight?

He could add in his head and could measure something just by looking at it. He knew exactly how much of a tree would fit into his pickup when the wood was split into firewood and exactly how many bushel baskets would go in that truck bed and exactly how many beans it would take to plant one row and how much ground sausage to put in the bucket to make five pounds or two pounds. Even though his illiteracy was a hardship for him, it defined him as a person. We kids grew up trying to get his attention by telling him things we thought would bring wonder to his face. Stuff we learned at school that we knew he didn't know about. He was surprised when I explained to him that the earth revolved around the sun. He couldn't get over it. All he knew was that when he got up in the morning, there was the sun and as the day went by, there went the sun until it disappeared, so he thought the sun was moving, not the earth. From the fruit bowl, I used an orange for the sun and a walnut for earth.

He could sound out some letters and could write his name and could even leave a short note for Mama on occasion. *Gon to get pig* (which translated meant gone to the beer joint) or *get gas* (which translated also meant gone to the beer joint).

When we were growing up, getting his attention was a real treat. It wasn't that he didn't love us, he just didn't know how to relate to us outside of showing us how to plant a garden or milk a cow. I can't ever remember him engaging in play with us. Discipline was entirely Mama's job. If we were noisy he would just walk out and go to the garden or the barn. If we were rowdy in the back seat of the car he would say Boob can't you get them kids to be quiet? He called her Boob, which had nothing to do with boobs, it was just his abbreviation for Beulah Mae.

I think a lot of the time he didn't try to communicate because he was afraid of making a fool of himself. But he delighted in trying to teach us something he knew. He would say Come here I want to learn you something. He didn't have much patience during the teaching process. You either got it the first time or pretended you got it. Then he would come along behind you and say you were doing it wrong. He expected us to be as observant as he was and pick up on things right away.

He was a master at ingenuity and gerryrigging when it came to getting a job done. He would try one thing and then another until he figured out how to get it done, whether it was moving a 250 pound hog or felling a fifty-year old oak tree beside the house. He had his own ideas about how such things ought to be done and rarely ever listened to any advice from anyone. Sometimes he would attempt really dangerous things over the objections of my mother and everyone else. She would say Posey you're going to kill yourself or You're going to put that tree down in the middle of the house. He would ignore all advice and go ahead with what he was doing. What was maddening to my mother was that it usually worked and he would come out of it unharmed and laughing. It gave him enormous pleasure to show everybody that he was right after all.

I have heard him say too many times to count that he wished he had had an education. I was probably fifty years old before I realized that wasn't true at all. He never regretted anything he ever did or didn't do. It just wasn't in him. He had too much ego and stubbornness. Ego is a big word to use in reference to him because you would never think of a person who couldn't read as having an ego. Mama's efforts to teach him after they were married were futile. When we were growing up, we tried to teach him to read but he just didn't have the patience.

We had always thought it was because there were so many children in his family and they lived in the hills of Virginia and there were no school buses and they were poor. But his younger brother Harding told us he would be dropped off at school by the older kids and as soon as they were out of sight, Daddy would light out for home. So there was some effort by Grandpa and Grandma Wright to get him to go to school. They probably gave up after a while and let him have his way. Stubborn is a word that defines Daddy exactly. Stubbornness and determination. My friends know exactly where I get it from.

Chapter 15

Reading

 $\mathcal{M}$ ama, on the other hand, loved to read and it was in this way that she educated herself over the years. She loved mysteries and Maeve Binchey. I shared her passion for reading, and like her, I could immerse myself in a good book for hours. Housework and chores were done by working for thirty minutes to be rewarded by fifteen minutes of reading. Good books were treasured and the ultimate luxury was being able to have a good book going and another good book waiting to be read.

After they both retired, Mama carried her paperbacks along when she went with Daddy into the woods for the day to cut up firewood or when she went along with him on any of his various excursions and had to wait in the truck. Daddy never understood this love of reading and often complained about her always having her nose in a book. When he came into the house from working outside, she was expected to lay down her book and listen to whatever tale he was telling. His tales were always about the same things. The sick pig or the new batch of piglets or how the vegetables in his garden were growing or not growing, the lack of rain or the lack of sunshine, the stupidity of one of his cronies, the laziness of a fellow construction worker, his truck or his tractor and on and on. Mama always laid her book down and listened to his tales, trying to be interested, secretly wanting him to go back outside so she could go back to reading.

I bought used paperbacks by the bagful from the Book Exchange in Chesterfield County for about the last ten years of her life. Mama's eyes would light up when I came in the door with a grocery bag full of new books. We would split them up, she'd take half and I'd take half and after we read them, we'd swap. She had a way of grading them and would put her pencil mark on the first page, and I knew if it was a P for poor, I didn't have to waste my time.

Mama was the kind of person who wouldn't give herself permission to sleep past seven or eight o'clock in the morning until she was almost eighty years old. Then she said there wasn't all that much she had to do every day so why not just sleep in a little. She would often read until 2:00 in the morning because at that time of morning she could get some peace away from Daddy. So when she would be up that late, she would sleep in until maybe 9:00 the next morning.

She also loved good movies and *Murder She Wrote*. One of the things we liked to do best in the last years of her life was go to movies together. Friday nights, we would eat at the cafeteria in the mall, always the same thing, fried fish, spoon bread with at least three patties of butter on top, mashed potatoes and gravy and iced tea. After dinner, we would go to a movie. She always told me to pick the movie because we liked the same kinds of movies, dramas or who-done-its.

When she went on oxygen twenty-four hours a day, we would still go to the movies and she would sit on the aisle, tank at her feet. I think the last movie we saw together was *The Apostle* with Robert Duval and it was a great disappointment. We both loved him in his movies and for once she picked a movie that she wanted to see. About an hour into the movie, she had to go to the bathroom. She had to have help with her tank and I had to go along to keep her steady on her feet. On the way back to our seats, she said If you're not enjoying this movie, I wouldn't mind leaving. I had not said a word about the movie. It was her way of telling me she wasn't enjoying it, so I got our coats and we left.

There were a few times when we went to movies with her in a wheelchair. I would call ahead to the theater to see where the handicapped entrance was located and would wheel her into the theater and park her chair in the aisle in the back.

Over this period of time, the moviemakers seemed to have a certain formula for every movie and one of the parts of the formula was at least five minutes of sex. We liked it when the sex scenes came at the beginning of the movie and we would whisper to each other Well now they can get on with the movie with the sex out of the way.

Mama had a dry sense of humor and it was hard to find anything that made her laugh. She grinned a lot if you were telling her a funny story and sometimes when there was a fart scene in a movie, her shoulders would shake with laughter but she rarely ever laughed out loud. She didn't get the humor in a lot of movies and thought most of them were just silly. She loved a good joke, even dirty ones, but didn't know how to tell a joke at all, whereas Daddy was the best joke teller there ever was. He had the timing, the country way of describing a situation, and the mannerisms, and would deliver the punch line while pounding on his knee laughing and you got as much good out of his laugh as you did the joke.

But Mama got a kick out of some of the things Daddy did and would often begin a conversation about one of his escapades by saying Let me tell you what your Daddy did. There was plenty of fodder for these tales because Daddy jerryrigged most everything and thought you could build anything as long as you had a piece of wire and some old boards and a few nails. He amazed all of us with the contraptions he would rig up, from fences for his pigs to trellises for his cucumbers.

He constructed failsafe supports for his tomato plants by cutting the bottoms out of plastic milk crates that he got from the dairy. The milk crates would hold four gallons of milk and he amassed hundreds of these plastic crates from his trips to the dairy to get expired milk to feed to his pigs. He would cut the bottom out of the crate and as the tomato plant grew up inside the crate, he would stack the crates on top of each other until the plant finished growing and started to produce little green tomatoes. This ingenious method allowed the tomato plant to get sunshine and rain while stabilizing the vines and also allowed you to pick the tomatoes from the open top.

She laughed at some of his contraptions and at the same time you could tell she was proud of the way he would come up with a solution that worked. His method for solving problems was always unorthodox. If a thing didn't work the way he thought it should, he would just find another way to get it done.

Mama was of the school of if at first you don't succeed, try, try again. Her philosophy had more to do with never giving up on your dreams while Daddy's was just bull-headed determination to win out. Just a slight difference in frame of mind, really.

She had enormous faith in God. She didn't spout religion, though, as some Christians feel they must. There were no Praise the Lords or admonitions about sinful life. She just lived her faith in her everyday life and approached all problems knowing she would find the way with God's help. Having Daddy as a husband would have put a trial on anyone's religion and I didn't realize until very late in her life just how much she had relied on her faith to get her through some of the things Daddy did.

Writing about it now after Daddy's death, I have a tendency not to tell the whole truth because I came to accept him more as he was rather than being resentful for what he was not. That did not change or excuse his behavior of the past, but I came to believe that he was just doing the best he could and didn't know how to tell us he loved us except to work hard and provide us a home. I also expect that by this time I had come to know a lot of men who were just like him.

It seemed to me that he broke my mother's heart in many ways. There was philandering with other women all of their married life. I realized Daddy paid a lot of attention to women even when I was very young. When he was eighty-three he was still paying a lot of attention to women. The thing of it was, he really thought he had a chance. Even when he smelled like pigs or garbage and had nothing whatsoever to offer a woman, it didn't slow him down one bit. He thought he was charming them to death and it never occurred to him to think otherwise.

His philandering always involved drinking and it was always with trashy women, the kind who hang around beer joints for the attention of the men who were always there drinking. I never knew of any one particular woman, but there were many instances of him and his redneck buddies having parties and continuing to drink at someone's house after the beer joint closed and these parties always involved women. He would always say that he was just having a beer and if Mama didn't believe him why didn't she come with him.

So Mama began to go with him and would sit in a booth and talk to some of the other people there, some waitresses or some of Daddy's friends. She never drank because she didn't like the taste of alcohol or beer but would have a coke or a cup of coffee and would try to pass the time while Daddy got drunk. She started out doing this because she could drive him home but he never wanted to leave when she did, so she ended up driving her own car and would have to leave and go home knowing he would be driving home drunk again. Some people would call this enabling and it probably was but it was only one of the many things she tried in her relationship with him trying to find a way to make it work better.

One night when she was on the way home from the beer joint, a cop stopped her and gave her a ticket for an expired inspection sticker (which was Daddy's fault for putting off getting it inspected) and she was so incensed at this injustice that she told the cop he ought not to be stopping people for expired stickers but ought to be watching for drunk drivers and if he waited a few minutes, he would see a drunk driver coming along. Sure enough, a few minutes later Daddy came down the road driving his truck and he was, in fact, drunk. The cop followed them both home but did not give Daddy a ticket, which was how it usually went.

After many years of trying one way after another to change his drinking habits and make him stay home, she finally gave up and left him alone. It took many years of heartache and worry on her part before that happened. There were times when she would call me when he wasn't home yet and the beer joint would have been closed for some time and we would go out looking for him, half afraid we would find him dead on the side of the road. But usually he was passed out in his truck in the parking lot of the beer joint or sometimes we would go looking for him at some redneck's house. If we found him in his truck, parked in the beer joint parking lot or in front of some redneck's trailer, we would just leave him because he would sleep it off and come home later. Mama wouldn't let me go to the door of the trailer to confront him, even though I wanted to. She'd say she knew where he was and that's all she wanted to know. Sometimes we wouldn't find him and she would call the county jailhouse and there he'd be. Once we got him out of jail but after that she would say Just leave him there, might teach him a lesson. It didn't.

He got a series of DUI tickets (Driving Under the Influence), at least twelve that I recall, over the course of forty years. He would have his license suspended and would have to get his lawyer friend to get it back. His lawyer friend was on the shady side and for a few hundred dollars, Daddy always managed to keep driving. Or he would attend driving school and because he couldn't read or write, Mama would have to attend with him. She said for a teetotaler, she was the most educated person in the world on the perils of not drinking and driving. She would also have to go with him to take the written tests. He didn't study because he thought it was all poppycock and the gov'ment meddling where they had no business and he wouldn't know the answers but he would fake it like he was thinking about the questions she read out to him and then she would answer the questions because she knew it backward and forward.

He never had a serious accident in all the years of driving drunk. He backed his truck into a number of buildings and fence posts and the bumpers and fenders of his trucks were always mashed and battered, but he escaped doing himself or anyone else any serious injury. Maybe there was something to her prayers after all.

Daddy was a great procrastinator and put off everything until the last possible minute and then beyond that. This drove Mama crazy because she was a person who faced chores as things that had to be done so why not go ahead and do them and get them out of the way. Daddy wasn't so conscientious. He would go to great lengths to get around work he didn't want to do. Mama would say that if he spent as much time and energy doing a job as he did getting around it, he would end up with a whole lot of excess time. Their different approaches to life were the source of much argument and many battles. She would see that something she had reminded him to do hadn't been done and the reminders turned into nagging, then threats and finally ultimatums delivered through clenched teeth. It was the clenched-teeth stage that he finally paid attention to. I asked Mama one time why she didn't just start with the clenched teeth and she said Oh he would see right through that and then I might have to get violent to get his attention. This way works. It wears me out, but it works.

Daddy was also tight with a nickel. I would say tight with a dollar but that wouldn't be right. He was tight with every nickel. True story. There was a toll bridge across the James River in Richmond and Daddy had to cross through the toll twice a day to get to and from work. The name of the bridge was The Boulevard Bridge but it was known to everyone as the Nickel Bridge because the toll was a nickel. For people who used the toll every day, you could pay an annual fee for a small metal tag that was attached to the vehicle's license plate with a couple of screws. He kept the toll plate attached to his truck but on weekends if we had to go across the bridge for any reason that tag would come off the truck and would get attached to whatever car we were driving. To save a nickel. We kids were teenagers at the time and after we were grown, we used to relay to other people that example of how cheap he was, even in front of him, and Daddy would want to know what was so funny.

Being tightfisted was one of Daddy's main things. He would go to great lengths to repair something without buying the part or he would do without the part. If at all possible, when something had to be fixed at the house, like the roof, he would find one of his cronies to do it for free or in exchange for vegetables or some sausage. He had a friend who was a roofer but not a very good one, so their roof was the sorriest looking mess you have ever seen. Mama had to get things repaired on the sly because he would raise holy hell anytime she spent any money on anything.

The best things in Daddy's life were free. He would take anything anyone wanted to give him if it was free. And sometimes they were free without the knowledge of the owner. He borrowed things from places that stored things outside that weren't locked down. Whatever bale of wire or pile of wood or bucket of rusty nails he could pilfer, he did. And what wasn't free, he would haggle over in the store. He would exclaim My God almighty what do you mean charging that kind of price. You must think I'm crazy to pay them kinda prices. Mama would be mortified by embarrassment in the store. She would try to reason with him and he would fume and walk away. Sometimes she would go against him and buy it anyway and if it ever broke down, she would never hear the end of it. He was not one to hold back on I told you so. Most times she would just walk away from it unless it was something really, really necessary and sometimes she would buy it with her own money just to keep him quiet, but that didn't work either because he would go on and on about If that's the way you want to spend your money.

There were some things that it was beyond his comprehension that people would pay for. Taking trash to the county dump, for instance. Why pay to dump trash when you could just throw it in somebody's dumpster, or better yet, burn it behind the pigpen on the hill, ignoring there was an ordinance against it.

Because he was so tight-fisted, my mother was brainwashed

into the same kind of behavior and it was also learned by me and my siblings. The philosophy that nothing was ever wasted was taken to the extreme. I would find myself examining a plastic bag or piece of aluminum foil to see if it could possibly be used one more time. It was just a few years ago that I told myself to put this thing in prospective, for Pete's sake, it's a plastic bag.

Chapter 16

Things Wendy Remembers

*M*y daughter Wendy was born in 1965 and Mama came to the hospital soon after I started in labor and refused to leave until Wendy was born twenty-four hours later. Years later, after Wendy was grown and married and had a daughter of her own named Sydney Nicole, I remember watching Mama sitting at her treadle sewing machine stitching up the patches to make Sydney a quilt. At that time, Mama was on oxygen twenty-four hours a day and had to sit at the sewing machine with the oxygen tube over her shoulder while she sewed. As I watched her sewing, I remembered her vigil with me in the hospital.

As soon as she could talk, Wendy began to call Mama by the name that came out of her mouth instead of Grandma, which was Meemaw. Mama became Meemaw from that day forward to all of us, her grandchildren yet to be born or adopted, her great- grandchildren and even to Daddy.

By that time, Johnny and I had divorced. We parted as friends and have remained friends. In this book I call him Johnny of a few words because that describes him well. He was quiet and even withdrawn, speaking his opinion very rarely. When he did speak, it was usually a jewel. We divorced in 1966 and when Mama died, Johnny of a few words sent a card which said all the words that could ever be said about her: She was a good woman. After we divorced, I moved into an apartment in Richmond, close to Mama and Daddy. Later, I moved into the house on Warwick Road where Wendy and I grew up. In other words, I grew up as Wendy grew up. I never remarried.

While we were living on Warwick Road, Wendy started school. When she turned nine, children living within the city limits of Richmond were bused out of their communities to satisfy racial integration in the schools. So that she would not have to ride a bus to the North side of Richmond for one hour, I registered Wendy as living at Mama's house, which was, at that time, in the county. Wendy got off the school bus in front of Mama's house and stayed with Meemaw until I picked her up after work. Some days she and Mama would watch soap operas on television. Mama called them stories. They both knew that I thought these stories had very few redeeming qualities, so they kept it a secret until Wendy giggled and gave it away. She and Meemaw formed a special bond and no one and no thing ever got between Wendy and her Meemaw.

Wendy remembers going with Mama to Elaine Powers at Southside Plaza to take exercises. There was a Woolworths next door to Elaine Powers and Mama would give her about $1.00 and she would go over to Woolworths and buy stuff while Mama was taking exercises. The S&W Cafeteria was also at Southside Plaza and during the summer when there was no school, Mama would take Wendy with her when she sold or delivered vegetables to the S&W. She would have a trunk full of green peppers and tomatoes. Daddy went to all the local restaurants, going in the back through the kitchen, making arrangements with the cooks to buy his fresh vegetables. He would load them up in Mama's car and she would deliver them and collect the money and keep track of how much money they made all summer. It was in the neighborhood of $3,000. A bushel of tomatoes was about $5.00. Green peppers were about $3.50. A lot of trunk loads of vegetables.

When Wendy was much smaller and Mama would baby sit, Mama would take Wendy with her to the bar where Daddy was drinking beer. Mama's friend Nell would come there and join them and have a beer and Mama would have coffee. Wendy remembers standing up in the booth and was barely able to see the people in the next booth. Wendy said she remembers playing in the booth with her Barbie dolls. It cost a quarter to play the pinball machine and Daddy would play and bet on the games and sometimes win a lot of money, sometimes lose a lot. Mama was never allowed to scold Daddy for gambling because he said he worked hard for the money and sold vegetables to make extra money so it was his to gamble with. Never mind that Mama had planted the seeds, tended the weeds, picked the vegetables and sold them herself. She wasn't foolish enough to gamble away anything so hard won, but her vote didn't carry much weight when it came to playing pinball. When it looked like it would get out of hand, Mama put her foot down. But per Posey's orders, any discussion about gambling up to that point was verboten because it would affect the winning streak, if there was one.

Mama used to hide money in the Bible and when Wendy, looking for the pretty colored pictures in the Bible would find money, Mama would say Shhh don't say anything and would turn the page.

Chapter 17

Sausage

During all the years while they lived on Ruthers Road, when Daddy was hanging out at the beer joints, he would always invent an excuse to get away from the house to go drink beer with his cronies. He had to see a man about some pigs or he had to look up so and so and see about getting his truck fixed or it might be he would be looking at a truck to buy. Mama would say Well there's the phone, why don't you just call. He didn't have the man's number. Mama knew what he was up to and knew he would get around her questioning and knew she was wasting her breath but for many years she gave it her best shot. The most telling thing about his made-up stories was he would wash up and change to clean clothes before he left the house.

Long after she stopped caring about his excuses and had gotten to the point where she wanted him out from under her feet so she could have some peace, he continued making up these bald-faced stories of why he had to "go down the street." She would say Posey go on and go wherever you want to go, you don't need to make up some lie about it. But he continued to come into the house to wash off before he went to the beer joint, telling some tale the whole time he was getting cleaned up about why he had to go see so and so. It was by this time a ritual that was part of the process and he couldn't seem to change the pattern after all those years.

One of his valid reasons to go down the street was to peddle sausage, which he pronounced sotchage. Three or four times in the winter, he would butcher one of his big sows and make sausage. Butchering was done on the weekend because Doris and I would have to help and we worked during the week. Doris and I lived in Richmond and were right at hand; Harless lived in North Carolina and Nancy lived in South Hill, Virginia, a couple of hours away, so they were not pressed into service as often. There were a few occasions when some of Daddy's redneck friends would help out but this rarely worked out. They didn't show up at all or showed up still drunk from the night before or showed up thinking it was a lark to help the old man butcher a hog. They had never seen it done before and they were curious about it or they were taken with the novelty of it. But they found out quick enough that it involved a lot of work and Daddy didn't put up with any nonsense. You either pitched in and did what he told you to, or he would tell you to get the hell out of the way. Daddy was the one in charge and he gave the orders and you did exactly what he said or you got cussed. One guy showed up with a radio so he could listen to the Skins game but that only lasted about thirty minutes before Daddy told him to turn that damn noise off.

Daddy had his own way of doing things. There was the right way and the "Posey Wright" way, as my brother-in-law Oscar used to say. You didn't step up and make suggestions. He didn't need anyone's advice and got mad if you even tried to do it any way other than the Wright way. Never mind that you were giving up your weekend or that sometimes you would be standing around waiting for instructions. There were many jobs to do and after you had done it dozens of times as I had, you knew what there was to be done but you learned to wait until he gave the word before you proceeded or he would get irritated.

Out back of our house, there was a screened patio with a concrete floor and a three-foot brick wall with screen the rest of the way to the roof with a barbeque pit at the end of the patio. When we were teenagers we used to have parties out there with our friends in the Methodist Youth Fellowship group.

After we were grown, the patio was rarely used except for storage, so Daddy used it as his place to make the sausage. He put in two long shelves running the length of the patio on each side and these were covered with long sheets of plastic in preparation for the butchering. After the plastic was put down, the sausage mill had to be cleaned and the buckets and plastic bins and the knives made ready. Daddy would have sharpened the knives the night before on his grindstone or using a handheld file. The knife sharpening was a thing that Daddy made sure was done right because you couldn't cut up the meat with dull knives.

Cleaning the parts to the sausage mill was Mama's job. The grinding arm and all the blades had to be hand washed in very hot water and wiped clean of any moisture so they wouldn't rust. She was also responsible for gathering the buckets and pails and cleaning them and for getting the sheets and clean rags ready. Daddy would take his tractor up on the hill where the hogs were, with a crane and chain hitched to the back of the tractor. He would park the tractor close to the pigpen where he had prepared a holding area for the sow and he would get in the pen and separate the sow from the rest of the hogs and put her in the holding pen. He would shoot her with his 22 rifle between and just above the eyes, usually one shot, because he knew exactly where to place the shot and the sow would drop where she stood.

Daddy would attach a brace between her hind legs, bind the legs with chains and hoist her up into the air behind the tractor, head down, nose almost touching the ground. Then he would make his slow way back down the hill to where we were waiting in the patio behind the house. Sometimes the sow was so big that the front of the tractor would rise up with the weight and anybody else would be frightened of the consequences but Daddy would just keep on ratcheting the sow up until the weight leveled out and the front end of the tractor would settle back to earth. While he was making his way down the hill, the sow, bleeding from the head, would sway back and forth on the back end of the tractor. Daddy just kept coming and only occasionally would he even look back over his shoulder, maybe if he was passing under a low-hanging tree branch.

He would back the tractor up to a big tree next to the patio and use a pulley attached to a big limb to hoist the sow to a hanging position on the limb. From this position, hanging from the tree limb, Daddy would skin the hog. Many years before, he would scald the hair off by putting the hog down in a barrel sawed in half and filled with boiling hot water. He determined that way was too hard and devised his new method of skinning the hog. After he got the hog hanging from the tree limb and stable, he would cut down the belly of the hog from one end to the other, removing all the organs and putting them aside for more workup later. Then he would hose the hog down and skin it.

Under the tree, he arranged four sawhorses with a sheet of plywood on them and then an old bed sheet on top of the plywood to keep the meat clean. It was a tricky job at this point to remove the hog from the tree limb, back the tractor up and lower the hog onto this piece of plywood. He had to get the hog in the middle of the plywood so it wouldn't fall off the platform and only with a lot of patience and skill would anyone at all be able to lower a 200-pound slab of meat onto a moveable table, but he did it, time and again. By himself. Telling me the whole time, Get out the way, get out the way, as I stood by uselessly looking on. I finally learned to get out the way and go inside the patio where I didn't have to watch.

Once he got the carcass on the platform, he used his knives, hatchet and saws to separate the hog down the middle in two halves, one line on each side of the backbone, remove the backbone and cut up the remainder of the hog into six pieces, two hams, two shoulders, and two pieces of middlin' meat. As he finished carving up each piece, he carried it into the patio and placed it on the shelf where Doris and I would cut it further into fist-sized pieces and pile it high into a long ridge of cut up meat. All of it went into the sausage, the hams, the shoulders, all of it. All except the tenderloin. Daddy carefully carved out the tenderloin and later Mama would fry it for breakfast and tenderloin sandwiches. After Doris and I cut up the meat into smaller pieces, Daddy decided how much seasoning was needed and boxes of sage and sausage seasonings were mixed together and spread over all of the pieces. Daddy mixed it with his hands, going up and down the shelf mixing it and turning it over and over. Once he was satisfied it was well-mixed, the pieces were fed into the sausage mill. The ground sausage was caught out of the sausage mill in an oversized dishpan and put back on the shelf where Daddy mixed it up some more to distribute the fat. The mound of ground sausage on the shelf would be a foot high and ten to twelve feet long. He would then start at one end of the shelf and scoop up what he thought was ten pounds of sausage, put it in a bucket, and hang the bucket on the scales, which were hanging from a cross beam in the middle of the patio. Eight out of ten times, there was exactly ten pounds of sausage meat in the bucket. He'd grin and say Looka there would you, just looka there, and then he'd grab the bucket off the scales and dump the meat in another pile where I would wrap it up for him to sell.

He sold it in ten, five and two-pound packages at $2.00 a pound and didn't really make much of a profit, but it was his thing and he was widely known for making good sausage. It was a matter of knowing how much sage and seasoning to mix with the meat and even though he used amounts of seasonings based approximately on the amount and weight of the meat, he had a knack for knowing when to add just a little more to make it right. After he finished mixing, he would send one of us to the house with a sample sausage patty and Mama would fry it and send it back to him to test. Two hundred pounds of sausage provided lots of opportunities to "go down the street" to sell the sausage.

The hog butchering could be a two- or three-day affair, depending on the weather and if it was cold enough to leave the meat outside overnight so you could finish working it up the next day. The perfect temperature was above freezing so the meat didn't freeze but cold enough to keep it from spoiling. It was much easier for us to cut the meat after it had cooled off overnight, but it was hard on the hands to work with cold meat. I preferred to work with the meat while it was still warm and get it all done in one day. Which is what we did the last few times Daddy butchered a hog. We got to the point where we preferred to do it alone, just the two of us, and we'd be dead tired at the end of the day because we would work from early morning until very late at night, but it would be done.

Daddy had been making sausage and selling it to his neighbors and friends for many years and each year he would have advance orders from repeat customers. Mama was in charge of keeping track of who wanted sausage and how much. People would start calling him in September and October to get their orders in. When he had orders for as much as fifty pounds, he would start telling Mama, I got to butcher a hog here soon. Doris and I would groan.

Chapter 18

The Phone Book

$\mathcal{T}$he numbers for all of Mama's contacts were in the black Phone Book. It was an address book that Mama kept in a flat basket on the table beside her recliner (along with her inhalers, dental floss, Daddy's nail clippers, her Daily Devotional, some shotgun shells because Daddy wanted them close by if a pack of stray dogs got into his pigpen, and various ointments for Daddy's cuts and lacerations).

The Phone Book had to be replaced every couple of years because it got worn out from so much use. In it were the numbers for the stock pen where Daddy took his hogs to market, the dairy where he picked up outdated milk and ice cream to feed to his hogs, the two or three beer joints where Daddy hung out, numbers for places where he got parts for his truck and had chainsaws repaired, and past and present sausage customers.

Also the numbers for the pig farms who sold small pigs that Daddy would buy and raise to market weight, nurseries that would grow seedlings from Daddy's tomato and green pepper seeds, the pharmacist at Ukrop's drugstore that provided Mama's many drugs, Mama's several doctors, her preacher and the addresses for her seven brothers and sisters and her children and grandchildren. There were numbers for Daddy's cronies and men he hunted with. They had names like Shorty and Junior and Sarge and Buddy and Slim. There was even a number for the county jail. The Phone Book was a list of their lives.

Daddy never looked up a number in The Phone Book. He would just come in the house from the garden or pigpen and tell her to get him the number for so and so and she would reach for The Phone Book. She would look up the number and would usually dial it for him. The last Phone Book was so well used that the front cover had fallen off. On the front page in large bold handwriting were the work and home phone numbers of the three daughters and 911 HELP, for Daddy's benefit in case Mama wasn't there or in case something happened to Mama. Under "E" in large letters was written EMERGENCY ELECTRIC 888-667-3000 IN THE EVENT OF POWER GOING OUT, MAMA IS FIRST ON LIST TO BE RESTORED - WE HAVE LETTER ON FILE AT VEPCO. This note wasn't for Daddy's benefit; it was for anyone who happened to be there if the electricity went out because Mama's oxygen supply was electric.

In this book were also the addresses of my best friends. I had three best friends, Alice and Joyce and Jean, and my mother loved them all and sent them Christmas cards every year. I was so proud because my mother liked my girlfriends. It was my boyfriends that caused her concern. I remember one time my daughter Wendy brought a boy to our house for the day to meet me and he had tattoos and earrings and looked like a hood. As soon as they left, I got in the car and drove to Mama's house and apologized to her for every scruffy, ragamuffin derelict I had ever dragged home.

Chapter 19

Daddy's Words

*D*addy had a way of fracturing the English language, much like Archie Bunker on *All in the Family*. Because Daddy could not read or write, he didn't know how words were spelled. He would repeat words he had heard someone else use and pronounced them the way he heard them. This meant that he often left out the first letter of the word, as in *ambunctious* for rambunctious. He would substitute sounds at the beginning of words, as in *consume* for assume or *barclay* for broccoli. His pronunciation of these words became our pronunciations within the family. When he was saying goodbye to us, he would say *adirosy*, which was his way of saying adios. We kids still say adirosy when saying goodbye to each other. Or he would misuse certain words.

One day Mama was watching television when he came into the house. He had a habit of doing that, coming in in the middle of a show and no matter what she was doing, he would start in telling her what was on his mind and he expected her to stop and listen. Besides, he thought TV shows were silly and the actors were *eejits* and he never watched anything on TV except animal shows or Bluegrass music. These he would tolerate because he loved watching animals, especially baby animals, and liked animals in general even though he was lackadaisical about caring for his own. He was raised hearing Bluegrass music, so there wasn't any other kind for him, all the rest was just noise.

When he came in, he sat down in his chair and started speaking to Mama as if she had been just sitting there waiting for him to come and tell her a tall tale. Mama continued to watch her TV program hoping he would give up and go away. After several minutes, he realized she was still watching the program, so he got up and stood in front of the television and said Damn it, don't you know I'm trying to get your *attraction*.

If you caught him staring into space and spoke to him he would say Hush a minute, I'm *studying* about something. If somebody made a mess of a job, he would say he *mommicked* it up. A direction was not East or West but *over yonder*. He pronounced itch as *each* and said *I reckon* for I suppose so.

He sometimes substituted words for situations and we would hear them and say What did you say? Because the way he used it, it didn't make sense and even knowing how he would misuse words, we still couldn't puzzle it out. He would impatiently repeat the word as if to say Y'all are eejits if you don't know what I'm talking about and he would begin to explain what he meant. Take the word *matriculate*, for instance, a word I am sure he heard one of us use. He used it to mean a person did not understand something. They didn't matriculate. I suppose he had heard someone use the word misinterpret and got the two words confused. And even though we would say, Oh, you mean misinterpret, he would continue to say matriculate as if he knew what the word meant even if we didn't and we were obviously wrong. In other words, we didn't *matriculate* what he was saying.

His misuse of words was hilarious to Mama and she would often tell us You won't believe what your Daddy said today. She knew a lot of words by this time and could usually figure out which word he meant to use and she got a big kick out of it, but not in a mean way. She would talk about his latest word in front of him as if it was a good humor story and he would grin and laugh along with the joke, which of course meant that he would definitely misuse the same word again even though now he knew better.

When I was doing research on the history of language on the island of Okracoke on the Outer Banks of North Carolina, I discovered that linguists attributed the islander language and the words they used to the fact that they were isolated from the rest of society and therefore, the language had not changed. They determined that the language was derived from Old Elizabethan English, the same language used by all of the first settlers. As time passed, the language evolved and some of the original terminology was shortened, changed or dropped altogether; however, the isolated areas such as the Blue Ridge Mountains, Okracoke Island and Tangier Island continued to use the original language, and that is why today their usage is very foreign to the rest of us. It was during this research that I discovered the word *mommick*, which was one of the words used by the islanders, and was the same word Daddy had been using all along.

Chapter 20

Canning

$\mathcal{M}$ama canned everything that came out of Daddy's garden. We called it Daddy's garden but Mama worked in the garden just as much as he did. She loved to pick beans and tomatoes out of the garden in the early morning, before the sun made it too hot. Daddy was best at plowing the garden and laying the rows and showing us kids how to plant the tomato plants and seeds for beans and corn. He excelled in those things and could lay a perfectly straight row without any lines or guides. He wasn't as diligent, though, about keeping the garden weeded without Mama's nagging. She would have to threaten him sometimes that the weeds were going to take over the garden before he would do it. He didn't like to hoe, so Mama hoed around and between the plants and Daddy ran the tiller down the middle of the rows.

For a number of years, Daddy planted strawberries, enough so that Mama could can or freeze plenty for the family and still have a lot of berries left over, which Daddy would peddle to the local restaurants or to his buddies at the beer joints. The strawberries were extra large and juicy and he made extra untaxed dollars off of them. He put in a lot of time and work to grow the biggest, juiciest strawberries ever, and he became known as "Strawberry" in the neighborhood and at the beer joints. He eventually gave up the strawberry patch but the name stuck and people continued to refer to him as Strawberry into his eighties.

On the three acres behind our house in Richmond, two thirds of it was planted in garden. Tomatoes, October beans, string beans, cucumbers, green bell peppers, onions and squash went in the patch closest to the house. More beans, potatoes and tomatoes went in the patch further up the hill, and corn went in the patch at the very top of the hill. It really wasn't a hill, just land that was more elevated than where the house was, but Mama always referred to the uppermost area as "up on the hill." Up on the hill was also where the pigpens were. From the time we kids were young adults and Daddy was in his late fifties, Daddy raised pigs up on the hill. He bought small pigs weighing around twenty-five pounds at ten to twelve weeks old from farmers in Emporia and Smithfield and Petersburg, farmers not too close but not too far. He would put the piglets up on the hill and fatten them up and when they weighed between 175 and 200 pounds, he would transport them in his pickup truck, which had sides made from wire he had "found" or traded for, to the stockyard.

The stockyard was a place where beef, pork and veal was sold on the hoof to meat processing plants for sausage or hot dogs or bacon, and was bought by representatives from Oscar Meyer, Smithfield, Jimmy Dean. The pigs and other stock were auctioned off by the pound and Daddy's profit would be the difference between what he paid for the pigs when they weighed twenty-five pounds and what he sold them for at 200 pounds, which was sometimes substantial, since Daddy didn't put any money into the enterprise at all, save for the initial money he spent for the baby pigs. Daddy made arrangements with several local restaurants to haul off their garbage for free, and he would feed the garbage to his pigs and never have to buy pig feed at all. Or he would pick up outdated milk from dairies and outdated bread from bakeries. Except for his gas and time going around collecting this free pig feed, almost all of the money he got for the grown pigs was profit.

There was also another benefit to his picking up outdated milk and bakery products. A lot of this stuff was still usable, and in Daddy's mind why waste it on the pigs, so he would give stuff away to neighbors and friends. Unbeknownst to the receiver, this was a form of chattel that he would use later when he needed a favor from them in return.

There was much anticipation on his part when he had a bunch of pigs nearing the weight they needed to be for him to take them to market. He guessed their weight, of course, by sight and often challenged Mama to bet with him on the weight of a certain pig and Mama knew better than to bet with him, but would anyway, because he got so much fun out of it when she would guess the weight wrong and he guessed the weight right every time. It was Mama's job to call the stock pen to monitor the price of hogs so that Daddy could get the best price.

He would also breed his sows and raise their litters. He knew when the sow was ready to deliver and would make straw beds under the shelter for the sow and her piglets. It broke his heart when one would get crushed by the sow and he tried to save all the runts and would get down on his knees near the sow and hold the piglet to the sow's teat to help the runt get something to eat. He would want to bring them in the house where he could bottle feed them but Mama would not allow it.

The house and land were inside the city limits so who would think that anyone would be raising pigs on the back of their property inside the city. But there was a grandfather clause in the zoning that allowed the land to be used for agriculture and the clause would apply until the land was sold or passed to a new owner. Since the land was bought by Mama and Daddy in 1955, the grandfather clause applied to them and they could have cows and horses, or whatever agricultural pursuit they wanted. Betty, the next door neighbor, had a horse for a number of years but it was the pigs that brought the most controversy from the rest of the neighborhood.

When Daddy built the pens, there were no houses up on the hill in the area behind Daddy's garden or near the pigpens. Then developers began to build houses on every available space in Southside Richmond. In the fifteen-year period following my graduation from high school and moving away from home, the population of the area around our house tripled. As more and more houses, and then a school, were built on the land bordering theirs and adjacent to the pigpens, Daddy and Mama heard that the real estate agents were telling the prospective buyers that the pigs were only temporary and would be gone by the time they moved into their new home. Of course, Daddy had no intention of getting rid of the pigs.

By the time the new homeowners realized that the pigs were

not temporary after all, the real estate agents were long gone. The neighbors' only recourse then was to try to roust Daddy and his pigs out of the area. They banded together and lodged complaints with the city, county and state only to discover that the property owned by Mr. and Mrs. Wright was perfectly legal for raising whatever farm animal they chose.

That discovery did not deter the neighbors from pressing on with their mission of getting rid of Daddy and his pigs, and really, I couldn't blame them. Here you had put your life savings into a new home, near a good school for the children, and just over the fence in your back yard was a hundred pigs and their stinky pens. So they took the Wrights to court and lost, because the law was on the side of the Wrights. And so were we, the Wright family. We weren't proud of the fact that Daddy raised pigs, and we were as much in favor of getting rid of the pigs as they were, but we believed wholeheartedly that he had the right to do it if he wanted to and Mama and all of us stood by him, defending him against the neighbors. All of us, including Mama, knew that the harder they pushed, the more immovable Daddy would become. We also knew that as gross as the pigs were, it was his thing and to deny him his right would cause him to shrivel up and die.

He continued to raise pigs up on the hill, and at age eighty-nine, was still staggering up the hill to feed his hogs. When he became too weak, Nancy and I took turns after work and on weekends feeding the hogs. This went on for about a year after Mama died, until his dementia put him in the hospital in 2002 and from there, he went directly to Southerland Place, a nursing home equipped for Alzheimer and dementia patients.

It was only at this time when it became apparent he would never come home again that we contracted with a man to come and load the pigs up and take them to market to sell them. We never told Daddy, though, and we continued to make up stories about the pigs when we visited him in the nursing home. He was always concerned about his big boar hog and would continue to give us directions about having his hogs bred by his prize boar.

But I've gotten away from my subject. This chapter was supposed to be about Mama and canning. During the summer and fall, Mama canned. It was slow and backbreaking work and we kids always complained. Bushel baskets of tomatoes were brought from the garden to the porch, and then hauled into the kitchen where they were washed, blanched in boiling water on the stove, peeled, packed into cans and put into two pressure cookers, seven glass quart jars in each. Mama would have already washed the jars and scalded them in boiling pans of water. After the tomatoes were packed in the jars, a teaspoon of sugar went in the top of each jar, the lids placed on the jars and sealed, but not too tight. A metal holding basket went into the cooker for removing the jars once they were done. The cooker was filled with water, the jars of tomatoes placed into the holding basket and the lid to the cooker put in place and locked.

The temperature inside the cooker had to reach a certain point and remain at that temperature for a certain amount of time, so there was much monitoring of the gauge on the top of the cooker. Mama cautioned us over and over not to mess with the pressure cookers while they were on the stove. She needn't have worried about me, though, because I was deathly afraid that the top would blow off the cooker. I have not forgotten the hiss of the steam coming out of those cookers.

After the cooking was done and the cookers had cooled off, Mama removed the cans, one at a time, and they were transferred to the counter to cool off completely. During the cooling process, the lid would give a popping sound and Mama would know that the canning was a success and the cans could be carried to the basement. A small piece of masking tape was put on the top of each can with the year. Corn, October beans, string beans, squash, strawberries, beets, cabbage, carrots and sometimes even potatoes and sausage were preserved and stored in the basement for the winter. A concrete shelf in the basement, the length of the house and five feet deep, was stacked from back to front. There were four of us kids to help with the canning, but the bulk of the work was on my mother.

There were at least one hundred cans each of tomatoes and beans, and fifty or so each of the other vegetables. Mama and Daddy did this while working fulltime jobs, Mama as a cook in the school cafeteria and later as a seamstress in a garment factory and Daddy as a backhoe operator on a construction crew. Daddy got a charge out of counting the cans he carried to the basement and reporting these numbers to us. As the winter went on we were sent to the basement for a quart of tomatoes or a can of corn or beans. These vegetables would be transformed in the kitchen by Mama's hands into stewed tomatoes or creamed corn or October beans with sausage and we ate with gusto, which made it all worthwhile to Mama.

Interview with Mama's sister Christine, in her home in Salem, Virginia, August 2004:

I remember coming to the house in Richmond, there where she died. Us having such good times and always enjoyed coming to Beulah Mae's house. We always had such a good time and Beulah Mae always cooked up everything, had the best food. And clear 'til she died, she'd get up there and cook. You couldn't make her sit down. And then Posey, he would fuss. Every time we went, he'd fill our car up with stuff out of the garden, tomatoes and green beans. And he always kept the biggest onions for me, cause I loved onions so good and when any of the rest of them would go and I didn't, he'd find the biggest onion he could find and he'd say now I want y'all to take this onion to CHRISTINE now. We just always had such a good time and we sure do miss getting to come down there.

In the winter of 2004, after Mama had been dead three years and Daddy had been dead a year, I opened the last can of October beans while I was at the beach writing this book. The masking tape on top said '99. I cried as I ate them.

Chapter 21

Hats, Cats and Yard Sales

Daddy always wore a hat to hide his baldness. He had an assortment of hats that filled up the top of his closet and hung from every nail, door handle and chair rail in the house. Cleaning out his closet and disposing of his many hats was practically the saddest chore I had after he died. His hats were a part of him and as I went through them one by one, I remembered him wearing each one and what he was doing. He had dozens of baseball caps, some with flaps, made from heavier material for the winter, some with mesh for summer.

Our favorite of Daddy's hats was an old straw hat he wore in the garden. The straw on it was worn and sweat-stained and ragged around the brim. He wore it long after it should have been thrown out and when it threatened to fall apart, he patched it with duct tape. I bought him a new straw hat, nothing fancy, just a serviceable straw hat and he thanked me and put it in the closet and continued to wear the old one. We have many pictures of him wearing that old straw hat, tending to his cucumbers and tomatoes.

Everyone who knew him knew that he was bald but he was always embarrassed about his baldness and never let anyone see him without a hat. He even wore hats in the house and in other people's houses and into restaurants when we would occasionally get him to go out to eat. This embarrassed Mama and sometimes she would say For God's sake Posey, take off your hat, you're in a restaurant. He would usually do as she asked but he didn't like it one damn bit. Once when Mama talked Daddy into making a dress-up portrait of the two of them, he wanted to make the picture with his hat on. Mama said that was okay as long as they also made one without his hat. Then she just bought the one where he was without his hat. He had some nice dress hats for when he was forced to put on a suit or sport coat. When Mama and I went to Montana, she brought him back a nice suede dress hat. I kept it after he died because it looked good on him and I helped her pick it out.

As far as I know, he never ever bought a hat in a store. Hats were given to him by his children or Mama or friends or bought cheap by him at yard sales. He loved yard sales and thought that was the epitome of a good deal if you could buy a shirt or hat or pair of pants for fifty cents or a dollar. And he didn't just buy these clothes and stick them in the closet. He wore them. All of the clothes he bought at yard sales had been out of fashion for forty years but he didn't care one whit about fashion so it didn't bother him at all.

I remember him coming out once dressed in a pair of striped seersucker pants and with it he had put on a two-inch wide white leather belt. At the time, he was around seventy years old and the wide belt was something that would have been worn by a cool dude when it was in style twenty years before. Mama said Posey you're not really going anywhere dressed like that are you and he said Why sure. These is nice pants. What's wrong with them? Mama would just shake her head and say Lord have mercy. And then she'd say But Posey they'll laugh at you in that get up. Go change into something else, you've got some nice clothes in there. He would say I don't give a damn what them people think. And he would go on where he was going in his pants and belt that he wore only because he had gotten them cheap. After he got out the door, Mama said Now he's going to be telling anybody he meets that he bought those pants for $1.00. And then Mama would laugh and say Well, that's Posey.

He also bought shoes at yard sales for himself, us kids, and the grandchildren. By the time he got into his yard sale years, we were grown and had children of our own and could afford to buy our children good shoes. Nevertheless, he would drag home boots and shoes for us and of course they never fit and they would end up being put away in a closet. He was also famous for wearing the things he bought for himself even if they didn't fit. One time he bought a pair of dress boots, not work boots, dress boots. But work in them he did. About three months later, we found out just how ill-fitting those boots were when he took off his socks one day and his toes had become sore and infected from where his toes were jammed into the toes of the boots. He had never complained. He ended up having to be seen by the doctor to have the infection treated, over a $2.00 pair of boots.

He would bring home bikes and tricycles for the grandchildren that didn't work and would state that he was going to fix them up. These too got parked in the garage or basement along with his other clutter.

Daddy didn't much like dressing up and he especially didn't like washing up. He rarely submerged himself in a bathtub or shower but washed up in the sink, standing in front of it in his underwear. One time he had to go to the doctor about his foot and Mama ordered him into the bathroom to wash up. He came out of the bathroom carrying his right shoe and sock and started putting his sock back on his foot. Mama said What are you doing. He said What does it look like I'm doing, I'm putting on my sock. She said Don't tell me you just washed one foot. He said Well the doctor ain't going to be looking at that other foot. Why do I need to wash that one?

Another time, Mama had to go have her eyes rechecked for glasses and was in the bathroom brushing her teeth before she left for the appointment. Daddy came and stood in the bathroom door and asked her what she was doing. She said I'm brushing my teeth. Daddy said I thought you were going to the eye doctor.

Much later when he had to go to the nursing home, they told me the residents were bathed every other day and I remember thinking, Lord have mercy, how are they going to get him to do that. Much to my surprise, he submitted to his baths at the nursing home without complaint. Because he was so unsteady on his feet, the aide would have to help him in and out of the shower, which had a seat and he was able to sit down while the aide washed him. I think he enjoyed sitting there in the warm water, someone else tending to him, he didn't have to do a thing. For the first time that I could ever recall, there was no dirt under his fingernails.

He liked attention of any kind and people would gravitate to him. He could tell a story and a dirty joke like nobody else and people liked being around him and enjoyed his company. He was always good for a laugh and his buddies would tease him all the time about his curious ways and he didn't take any offense and would laugh along with them. Although I know there were times when he didn't understand why they thought the things he did were funny. He was just being himself and if they thought this was funny, then that was all right too.

He never missed an opportunity to brag on his children to other people. This usually occurred when we were being introduced to someone he knew. Along with the introduction would be an explanation of where we worked and what a good-paying job we had or we had our own office and could come and go as we pleased or we had just been promoted or we had a fine new home over in the ritzy part of town. This was his usual indirect way of telling us he loved us and was proud of us because he could never bring himself to say these things to us directly. I put this in the same category of him and Mama not being able to hug us. It just made him uncomfortable and he would have choked up saying things to us directly. I didn't say things to him directly either. I let Father's day cards say them for me. And Mama would read him the cards we kids sent him on Father's day and he would always cry.

Daddy had a bevy of cats he kept up on the hill at the pig-pens to keep the rat population down. He would pick up stray cats from the side of the road or would take any cats anybody wanted to give away. He named all of them and had several that he thought a lot of. He would come up on the back porch where Mama had her geraniums lined up in pots on the porch railing. The porch had a ceiling but was open to breezes. In the summer in Richmond, Virginia, however, there usually wasn't much of a breeze and when a breeze did come along, it was more like hot air being pushed around from one place to another. Daddy would come up on the porch to rest and study about things in between garden and pig chores. When he studied, he would be deep in thought and would have one of the tamer cats in his lap, petting it and talking to it now and then.

He had one cat that he found at the asphalt plant one day when he was there borrowing some stuff and of course he named her Asphalt. Asphalt slept in the shade on the porch and waited for him to come and talk to her every day, wrapping herself around his legs. I thought his heart would break when she was run over in the street in front of the house, but you'd not know it to look at him. He just cleared his throat real loud and said Well it's a cat, we'll get another. There was Blackie, Two Toes who had two white front toes, and a whole litter of solid white cats that roamed around up on the hill for a long time. He named them Whitey #1 and Whitey #2 and so on until finally there were too many and they all looked alike so they all became just Whitey.

Chapter 22

The Bet

We went to the Sutphin family reunion, Mama's side of the family, in Radford, Virginia, every Labor Day from the time I was a teenager. Daddy used to go with us but after we kids were grown, he would use the excuse that he had to stay home to take care of his garden or his pigs. Harless was in North Carolina, so it was the three girls and Mama making the trip from Richmond. We looked forward to the time in the car on the way there and on the way home.

We talked the whole way about what was happening in our lives and Mama would tell us stories about when she was a child or when she and Daddy were first married and we were children. Mama made us sausage biscuits to eat on the road and wrapped them in a dish towel.

The food at the reunion was cooked by my aunts, most of it being southern-fried and loaded with grease or baked and loaded with sugar. In other words, the best. Always, always, on the way home, our conversation would turn to the need for us to go on diets, especially Mama and me. Mama had inherited the Sutphin fat gene from Big Granny and I had inherited it from Mama. Mama was always encouraging me to lose weight. One particular time on the way home from the reunion, I suggested to Mama that we have a bet. A large bet. Maybe that would keep us on track. We discussed how much the bet would be and I said I wanted it to be a bet that neither of us could afford to pay so that we would stick to it. I suggested $1,000.00 and Mama nearly fainted. But she agreed. We decided on fifteen pounds over the next three months, the diet ending the day before Christmas.

Daddy thought it was funny and warned Mama she was going to have to pay me if she didn't lose the weight. He watched her weigh in and would ask her, in front of me, how much weight she had lost and would remind her that he had been looking at the scale when she weighed so she couldn't lie about it. It turned out we both lost our fifteen pounds so the bet was a draw, but I think Daddy was a little disappointed nobody had to come up with the $1,000.

Daddy was only five feet six inches tall and slight of stature while Mama was five eight and big-boned. Daddy's usual weight was around 150 and he never weighed more than 165 pounds at his heaviest, which was one summer when he voluntarily gave up drinking beer and discovered half-and-half; he drank it like milk. So he never got it why we were always worried about our weight. He ate vegetables and fruit, he actually liked them, whereas we craved potato chips and baked potatoes.

Mama, on the other hand, gained weight with each child and from a very early age, I remember Mama always being on a diet. She ate carrot sticks and celery and tried so, so hard to lose weight. She was never very successful though, and when she got cancer in 1994, she weighed over 200 pounds. It was a good thing she was overweight because she steadily lost weight over the next seven years. She finally reached her dream weight, about 135, a few weeks before her death. Like the last line in Hemingway's story, *My Old Man*, Seems like when they get started they don't leave a guy nothing.

Chapter 23

Plaque for 50th Anniversary

*O*n the occasion of their 50th wedding anniversary in 1988, we kids took Mama and Daddy out to dinner at The Fox Head Inn, a five-star restaurant that was housed in a Civil War-era farmhouse just outside Richmond. We presented a plaque to them that contained something written by each of the children. The things we had written were copied in calligraphy on a cream colored heavy weight paper and framed in a 14X16 gold leaf frame. My friend Jean was there for the occasion.

A Tribute to Fifty Years
January 22, 1938-1988

It is impossible for me to express how I feel about you. Thoughts of you always give me a warm feeling of joy, gratitude and thankfulness. I love you. Harless

It seems that I have changed a number of times while you two have always stayed the same. That solid sameness is my strength. I am what I am because of you. Janet

Thanks for forgiving us and loving us even when we broke your hearts. Thanks for letting us go and not interfering after we married. Most of all, thanks for staying together. Doris

Daddy - you taught me what real strength and true grit means. You showed me how to hang on until I succeed. Mama - you taught me how to pray, love God and respect myself. How can I fail? Nancy

Chapter 24

The Sewing Machine

 $\mathcal{M}$ ama taught us girls how to sew on her Singer sewing machine and we learned by her example after watching her make our dresses. She made curtains and quilts and Christmas stockings. She repaired Daddy's pants and altered the ones he brought home from yard sales that were way too long. She stitched up his shirts when he would get them caught in some piece of wire or on a nail. It was a Singer with a foot treadle and she could really go fast on it. She had large hands for a woman and long slender fingers and I remember watching her hold the two pieces of material together and feeding it in to the needle going up and down. When I took Home Economics in high school, they taught sewing and I already knew how to make dresses, but I learned things I had never seen Mama do, like mark with marking paper or pin up a seam before stitching it. After I learned all those things, I continued to sew like Mama had taught me, because by that time I could feed the material into the machine by sight, just like she did. It saved lots of time.

She sewed quilt pieces together on that sewing machine, and

made a quilt for each of us kids, I think it was Christmas 1999. She picked out the material, cut the squares, and sewed the pieces together with her oxygen tube thrown over her shoulder. Then my Aunt Edith quilted the pieces together. Mama kept it as a surprise for us, and I don't know how, because we were in and out of her house all the time. She had put the finished quilts into large green yard bags, so you couldn't see through them, and had Daddy bring them out when the time came to exchange presents. There was one with pink squares for Doris' Victorian bedroom, one with purple squares because that was Nancy's favorite color, one for Harless in blue, and one cream colored, for me, to match the colors in my spare bedroom. Daddy helped Mama pull the quilts out of the yard bags and grinned and grinned as he distributed the quilts, as if he had made the quilts himself. My quilt is now on a single bed in my spare bedroom/office, where I am writing parts of this book. The sewing machine is in here too. As I write, I reflect on the hours she spent at the sewing machine, making memories for us kids.

I can think of only one occasion in her life when I was able to do something for her to return some of those hours of sewing. Around 1990, I took up cross stitching and Mama asked if I would sew her something for the wall in her blue bedroom. She picked out the pattern which was of a rocking chair sitting on a front porch with a straw hat hanging on it and a quilt draped over the arm of the rocker. I deviated from the colors in the pattern and made the quilt in shades of blue to match the bedroom.

It took me three years to finish it. I worked on it at home

and took it with me when I had to travel for my job. I was doing a lot of traveling then and I would work on it on planes and in airports. It had been with me to Utah and Ohio and to California, twice. I wasn't very fast with the stitching. But it was finally finished and framed and signed at the bottom in cross stitching "for my mother." Mama sent me a thank you note which I kept in my briefcase until long after she died. The note is dated May 17, 1990. She wrote: *Janet, let me thank you again for the lovely picture. I know how many long hours you spent on it. When I look at it I think of all those little stitches and I can imagine love in every stitch. And that is a lot of love. No one ever went to that much trouble for me before. It came at a very opportune time. I shall treasure it always. It is my most prized possession because I know it was made out of love for me. Thanks again. I love you lots. Mama.*

Chapter 25

Mama's Hands/Daddy's Hands

$\mathcal{I}$ used to study Mama's hands while she was sewing. She held the two edges of the material together with her left hand, guiding it under the needle of the sewing machine, and used her right hand to keep the material steady on the backside of the sewing machine so it would go through in a straight line. If it was a heavy material and the weight of it would pull it down on the backside of the sewing machine, she would use both hands to hold the material together from the front. Her foot would pump the treadle and the machine would eat up large areas of cloth as she worked it under the needle. She would stop every few minutes to get another length of the material ready to be fed under the needle.

She never measured and she never used pins and very rarely did she have to rip out a seam and start over. She had a good eye and good hands. Her fingers were long and slim and big-boned and so strong-looking. And even though she did chores in the garden, they were always soft. It was such a comforting sound when she sewed. You could be anywhere else in the house and hear her sewing. The machine would go for a while and stop for a while and go again.

When we were kids, she used those long fingers to reach into the back seat of the car when we were being rowdy and would pinch whatever leg or arm she could grab. We would be scrambling back out of her reach, pulling our legs into the back seat, and leaning toward the windows when that arm extended over the back of the front seat and made a sweep. She didn't even look around. It was a pinch you didn't soon forget. It was very effective.

You noticed her hands when she was picking beans too. Her hands were big so she could hold a lot of beans in one hand. When I was a kid I remember her chastising me for picking one bean at a time and putting it in the basket. Look here, she would say, This is how you do it, watch me. And you wished she wouldn't be so good at teaching because it was more fulfilling to pick one bean at a time because then you could stall and make it last a long time. The longer you stalled, the less work you had to do and before you knew it, it would be time to go back in the house. It was no use though. She was onto that real quick. She would have no lingering, or groaning or whining. Everybody in this family pulls their own weight. When I started my first job when I was fifteen, I pulled more than my own weight. That got me high praise from my boss. It was a good philosophy to live by.

Strong is the word I would have used for my mother. Growing up, we kids thought she was the stronger one, over Daddy. She was the boss. She made the decisions, she laid down the rules, she meted out the punishment when the rules got broken. Years later, we disclosed to her that we thought she was by far the stronger parent, which shocked her. She said she had been bowing down to Daddy for years and years and how come we didn't see that. Little by little, it began to dawn on me that that was true. So in my forties, I began to see my mother in a different light and only then did I begin to learn who she really was.

Daddy's hands were exactly the opposite of Mama's. He had small hands but broad across the palm. Hands always dirty. Cuts and nicks on the tops of his hands, calluses on the palms. Dirt or grease always under his fingernails, from his jobs with Luck Construction or LeeHi Paving or working in the garden. Strong, capable hands when he would use a razor blade to castrate the young, male pigs. At first when I helped him do it, I had to turn my head because I was afraid he would hurt them. I held them down by holding onto their front legs while he did what he had to do with the bottom half of the pig. His ministrations were swift and true, though, so I learned to trust him and watched him while he worked.

He hated to wear gloves, they just got in his way, unless it was really cold. So his hands were always chapped and red. His hands were gentle though, when he would pick up one of his cats or one of the newborn pigs or when he picked up a baby. Gentle, careful, dirty hands. But it was okay that they were dirty. He was Posey.

Although Daddy appeared to be uncaring, he had a gentle and sensitive heart. He loved small children and small animals and handled both with cautious care. He would tear up when Mama read him his birthday and Father's Day cards or when he was talking about some trouble happening to one of the family or friends.

Neither of them used their hands to touch us kids. The saying

Never Laid a Hand On Us was absolutely true. Except when Mama would hold you still while she whipped you with a switch. There was never any hugging or caressing or rubbing your arm or any physical contact whatsoever. I admired their hands and what they could do with their hands and how much strength they had in their hands and it all came from their hearts.

Once, though, when Albert was about three years old, Wendy brought him up on the hill to see his Great-Granddaddy's pigs. Daddy was standing in the pigpen with the pigs moving around him at his feet. He was dirty from head to toe from feeding the pigs and working in the garden. Albert was squeaky clean, clothes just so, hair just so, cute little boy outfit that Wendy had probably washed out by hand. Daddy reached for Albert and Wendy handed him over with a little hesitation.

I know she was thinking what kinds of awful germs is this baby going to get on him from Granddaddy holding him. Daddy, grinning from ear to ear, took Albert up in his arms and talked to him gently and walked around the pen holding him, showing him the grunting, dirty, rooting pigs. Albert was not frightened because he was being held by Granddaddy, away from the threat of the pigs. Wendy was barely breathing. I was thinking, Wendy, just let it be for a few more minutes. Albert will probably get dirty but it's just dirt, it will wash off. And just once in my lifetime, I would like to have had Daddy hold me and talk to me like he was talking to Albert.

Wendy did exactly right. She didn't utter a sound and when Daddy handed her little boy back to her, she took him and inspected him for dirt without letting Daddy know.

Chapter 26

Warwick Road

$\mathcal{I}$n 1968 Mama made what she said was the scariest move of her whole life. She bought a brick house on Warwick Road about three miles from where she and Daddy lived on Ruthers Road. She had set up a savings account in her name only and had scrimped and saved her own money for years until she had $10,000. She put this down on the house and got a loan for the other $10,000. The deed was in her name only. She had talked with me and asked me would I rent it from her if she bought it. I said yes. I lived there eighteen years. She kept it secret from Daddy for a long time.

Wendy was three years old when we moved in and the years passed with many happy memories in that house. I fell in and out of love, Wendy grew up, we had family cookouts in the back yard and Christmas dinners in the dining room, birthday parties for Wendy and once a puppy under the tree. I went to work during the week and mowed the lawn on weekends, and mowed Mama's yard as well. Daddy worked hard in his gardens but mowing yards was not high on his list. I made a deal with him that I would mow their lawn if he would keep a lawnmower running for me to use. He kept his part of the deal about half of the time. If he didn't have one running, I would just go home and get mine.

Mama had bought the house she said as insurance so she would have somewhere to go if she ever left Daddy. She never spent one night in that house. But she always said it was there if she needed it. It was so close from my house to theirs that I could be there in less than five minutes. When she had her first heart attack in 1974, she called me and I broke speed records getting there. I don't remember where Daddy was. It was the middle of the night and there wasn't another car on the road. Now the lights operate twenty-four hours a day, but at that time, after it got late at night, the red lights would flash constantly instead of changing. I ran all of the lights. She was able to walk to my car and I raced her to the emergency room. She was in the hospital about a week. I spent the first two nights sleeping in a chair in her room until the doctor said she was out of danger. I remember I was dating a handsome German man named Horst Huetenhein who looked like Robert Redford and wore real leather pants and jacket, not because they were cool but because that's how Germans dress. He was born in Stuttgart and was a mining engineer in Pittsburgh. I met him on a ski lift at a ski resort in Pennsylvania. He came to visit me while she was in the hospital and we took her some gladiolas. Man was I ever stupid to let him go. Just thinking again about it now makes me wonder if I have any sense at all.

That was the first heart attack. Several years later, she had a second one and this time, it was Daddy who called. He was crying and he said You better come help your mother. Again, she made out all right afterwards. I was never too sure about the validity of the heart attacks because she was also diagnosed with a hiatal hernia which can feel exactly like a heart attack. At that time, tests weren't all that accurate or conclusive.

It was during the time I moved into the house on Warwick Road that I met my friend Jean. Jean thought Daddy was a stitch. She would laugh and laugh at the stories I would tell her about Mama and Daddy.

One time Daddy had to drive up to a cornfield in Hanover County to pick up some corn. The corn stalks had been cut down but there was some corn left on the ground and the man who owned the farm said Daddy could have the corn if he came in his truck and picked it up. Jean went with us. Daddy and Mama were in Daddy's truck ahead and Jean and I followed in my old Volkswagen station wagon. While Daddy was picking up the corn, Jean and I kept Mama company in the cab of Daddy's truck. Jean said to Mama, I bet he is the most fun to have around, does he just keep you laughing all the time? Mama answered her in her typical deadpan, dry voice, Oh yes, he's a real barrel of laughs. Which meant the opposite. Jean didn't know it but Daddy had narrowly missed being put in jail the night before because he was driving home drunk. And but for the leniency of the policeman, he wouldn't have been picking up any corn at all. Jean and I have revisited that conversation a hundred times and it's still funny.

It was also during the time that I lived in the house on Warwick Road that I met my friend Alice. In May 1983, I moved to the Outer Banks for the summer to get myself straight after going through selling my word processing business. I had spent the preceding three years pouring all of my energy and sanity into owning and running the small business and when I finally had to give up trying to save it, Mama said Take off for a while, get yourself straight, come back and try again. Mama was, as usual, in the background, cheering me on and dispensing the if at first you don't succeed mantra. So I packed my sandals, locked the house on Warwick Road, and moved to Kill Devil Hills, NC where I rented a trailer from a friend for the summer. Alice lived in the trailer next door. I moved into my trailer on Monday. I met Alice on Thursday. And like Posey Wright would say, that's all she wrote.

Chapter 27

Daddy's Trucks

From a very early age, I remember Daddy driving around in a Ford pickup truck. Always battered and banged up, sponge from the cushions in the front seat exposed, the dashboard dusty and cluttered with flashlights, screwdrivers, wrenches, rags, nuts and bolts, shotgun shells and sometimes eggs. When he had chickens up on the hill where the garden and sheds were, he would gather the eggs and put them on the dashboard of his truck. The eggs would stay put because there was so much other junk on the dashboard they wouldn't roll around. The eggs might stay there for a couple of days until he had at least a half dozen and then he would bring them in the house and hand them to Mama to put in the refrigerator, and he would be as proud as if he had laid the eggs himself.

The floorboard of his truck would be cluttered with spare parts, baskets of vegetables, fertilizer, seed packets, oil cans and more rags. On one occasion, the floorboard of his truck rotted out on the passenger side, but he didn't get it repaired or even cover the hole up, so you had to ride straddling the hole in the floor with the cold wind blowing up your leg. The doors would squeak loudly when you opened them and you usually had to slam the door real hard to get it to close. Old coats and hats and boots would litter the seat or would be stuffed behind the seat, along with his shotgun or rifle. Doris and I shared a long-standing joke that you should wear your worst old clothes if you were going somewhere with him in his truck because you were likely to get dirty just getting in the truck. When one of us would go with him somewhere, even just to ride up on the hill to see some new baby pigs, he would pull aside the old coats and rags and make a place for us on the seat and he would be a little embarrassed I think. But not much.

Sometimes the windows worked. Sometimes the door handles worked. Most of the time there were gauges that didn't work but he always managed to find a man at one of the service stations who would give him a passing inspection sticker. The service ticket would be made out to Strawberry. Some of the time even the gears didn't work. And all of the time, the truck was close to running out of gas. He never put more than five gallons of gas in his truck at any one time. He sometimes would carry a gas can along in the bed of the truck, but the can was usually empty. He rarely ran out of gas.

He loaded baskets of vegetables in the truck bed and firewood and huge garbage cans full of garbage for his pigs, so the truck was rode hard as they say in the country. About every two months, he would take a load of pigs to the stockyard in his truck. He would load the pigs by himself, six or eight of them, approximately 1600 pounds, until the tires were almost level to the ground. All of us would be saying You'll never make it, you're going to break down on the way to the stockyard with all that weight and he would laugh and pull out of the yard and never look back. He hauled his pigs to the stock market in pickup trucks for at least thirty years and I can only remember a couple of times when he would break down on the side of the road. Both times I think it was because of bald tires. He never listened to us about replacing his bald tires either. He would get a new tire only when he absolutely had to, exchanging one bald tire for a retread that was slightly less bald.

He drove with muffler pipes or other truck parts hanging from under the truck. He would drive right through the middle of town with a load of pigs without a second thought. He ignored weight restrictions and never washed the mud from his license plates and waited at least a week after the expiration to get his truck inspected. He thought state troopers and city cops were nothing but a nuisance, but if he was ever pulled over for any reason, he would charm the officers to death and would rarely get a citation. It drove Mama crazy because he defied logic and chance and reasoning and good sense, not to mention luck.

The springs were always shot from the loads he carried. He punished his trucks but they were Fords and built tough. He wouldn't own anything but a Ford. He proved over and over just how tough they were. I remember one time remarking on one of his trucks that was barely driveable, being held together with baling wire and duct tape. I said Isn't it about time you got a new truck? He said I'm going to drive 'er 'til she squats.

Never, ever were these trucks washed or waxed. Never. They were traded in for another used truck without soap ever touching their surface and with an unbelievable amount of mileage racked up on the odometer. He always got something as a trade-in toward the next truck and the new used truck would have a new first dent in it within a month. He didn't pay much attention when he backed up, and hit everything from pigpens to loading docks, once even hitting the side of the beer joint upon his inebriated exit.

He would drive at the searing speed limit of twenty-five or thirty mph even when he was stone sober. When he had been drinking, he went even slower. He ignored driving rules. He believed rules were for other people. Stoplights, for instance. He generally obeyed green lights, but he treated yellow and red lights as if they were a mere suggestion. Yield signs got the same amount of attention.

Loaded with pigs or not, he poked along. People behind him cussed as they passed and he would just say Oh go to hell or would give them the finger. He thought anything above forty-five or fifty mph was driving recklessly. As I got older, he would allow me to drive the family car on trips back to Radford and Christiansburg to visit relatives and he would sit in the back seat and drink cold beer out of his cooler and during the whole trip, he would be telling me to slow down, not to be driving like a maniac. I was probably doing fifty-five, the speed limit. He was a very vocal back seat driver. One time I was driving and was headed up a ramp onto the interstate. Daddy detested the interstate and would never drive on it himself because he thought driving at that speed was pure insanity and plus he would die rather than have to pay tolls. So he was already in a testy mood because I was taking the interstate and paying a twenty-five-cent toll. There were several potholes in the road and after I had hit three of them, he said Wait a minute, go back, you missed one.

Because he couldn't read, he relied heavily on Mama for directions. Quite often, though, he didn't pay attention when Mama was giving out the directions, so he was forever getting lost. She would sometimes have to repeat directions several times before he got it clear in his head where he was going, and she would remind him of landmarks to help him find his way. But if she was with him and would point out landmarks for future reference, he would say Yes Boob, I know where I am, what do you think, I'm stupid? He would go thirty miles out of his way not to have to pay a toll. He had a standing complaint with me because I would take the interstate and pay a toll to drive to the other side of town. I would get there twenty minutes faster than him and it would cost me less money, even considering the toll, because of the shorter distance. He was not convinced. Did I mention that he was stubborn?

Chapter 28:

Mama's Friends

𝒜ama retired on disability in 1974 at age fifty-five after having two heart attacks. All of us kids were grown, married, and in one case, divorced, by that time. When she retired, Daddy was sixty-one, and he didn't retire until almost ten years later. She had worked at a garment factory for about the last fifteen years before retirement and had made friends there, and she soon missed their company. She also began to focus on her lifelong effort to lose weight, and took out a membership to the Elaine Powers Exercise Salon, the first luxury she had allowed herself in her whole life. Not long after joining, she made friends with a group of women her age who also exercised at Elaine Powers.

Mama met Nell and they became friends and started exercising at the same time, so they could exercise together. Then two or three others started coming at the same time and eventually The Dirty Dozen was born. They were all retired or, at least, didn't work during the day and were all about the same age. In other words, wise to life with personalities and stories to match. Mama had not had any women friends since she was eight or nine, because after she and Daddy got married, she helped him on whatever farm they lived on, and there wasn't any time for friends.

The Dirty Dozen came into her life at just the right time. All of the women were at least high school graduates and had much more education than Mama. But they loved and respected her and some of them became lifelong friends. In particular, Nell and Margie became close friends and confidants. Nell's husband was named Ernest, who was a gregarious talker and Margie was married to Joe, whom Margie constantly chastised openly and lovingly. Like all best friends, Nell and Margie and Mama talked about their husbands and their children. These two friends became Mama's sanity check. She was always in awe of the fact that they were both so accomplished and marveled that they wanted to be in her company, even though she was a country bumpkin. She was especially close to Nell.

Interview with Nell Ellis at her home in Brandermill Retirement Center, Midlothian, Virginia, January 2008:

I started at Elaine Powers (an exercise and fitness salon) *in '73 when it was located there at the end of Ruthers Road and your mother lived on Ruthers. Elaine Powers moved over to Meadowbrook after that. We stayed a long time at Meadowbrook. And we would go to the Hardees there for breakfast after we exercised. Beulah would get a chicken biscuit and give me half of the biscuit. There was a bunch of men who came in there every morning to have coffee. They were retired too. About six of them.*

There were a lot of us and we would sit in a group and these guys got so they would move close to us so they could hear what we were saying. We became friends with a lot of them.

Beulah and I used to go other places together, have lunch or just shop and sometimes Ernest would go with us. Beulah used to tell me to leave Ernest at home when we went somewhere because Ernest would talk the whole time and she and I couldn't get a word in.

There were twelve of us when we started. We would go out to lunch for each one's birthday. That went on for a long time. And then Margie started going to Florida in the winter, and Shirley's husband was transferred to Pennsylvania, but Beulah and I stuck with it throughout. She would go to try to exercise even after she went on oxygen full time and stopped driving. I would go by there and pick her up and we would go exercise and then go get a biscuit and then I would take her home and help her back inside with her oxygen. She would not give up. She would go and get on that treadmill and it would be set at the slowest speed possible. She didn't give up, she just wouldn't give up.

Posey liked to talk too, to all of us. If he was up on the hill and he saw that one of us had come to visit, he would come down off the hill to talk. He would "perform" for us and Beulah would say Posey these people didn't come to see you, go on back up on the hill. I guarantee he and Beulah would get into an "exchange." Then he would turn around and go back up the hill.

She loved going to New England. She talked about the New England trip more than any of the other trips y'all took.

She used to bring Wendy to the exercise classes. She was just a little bitty thing. Little redhead. When she was keeping her you know, she would bring her with her.

We'd been friends for years and years but then it whittled down to where there was just Margie and me and Claire and Beulah. We would go up to Radford to visit Beulah's sisters and brothers and spend the night. Margie would usually drive and it was Margie and Beulah and me, and Claire went one time. And we would stay at Geneva's. One time Claire and I stayed at Fred and Edith's. In the evening, all of her sisters and brothers would come to Geneva's and we would go out and eat somewhere.

I'll tell you what I tell people when I talk about Beulah. She made a point to let everybody know she wasn't well educated. But I tell people she was the smartest and most well educated of anyone I ever knew. She educated herself. She read and she took notice of what people were doing. And she was a smart, smart lady. She really was.

One thing I admired about her, she protected Posey. She was his biggest protector.

She was real proud of her children. She was determined that all of you would be college educated and that goes back to her desire to get educated. She was real proud of all her children, she really was. Beulah was concerned sometimes about Nancy, like when Oscar died or when Doris and Garland got a divorce, she was worried a lot about them. I don't remember her discussing any problems you were having. I know she thought you were smart and I guess she figured you were okay to take care of your problems.

There's something else I remember about Beulah. Posey raised the vegetables but Beulah sold them. She had that trunk filled with vegetables. She would take…. like some restaurants would want a bushel of vegetables, she would take them to the restaurant after Posey loaded them up.

I thought a lot of Beulah, she was my favorite person. I think we were always close, but after it ended up just being the two of us, that was when Beulah was going down and I would go by and pick her up. Beulah was one of a kind, she really was. One of a kind. A special person.

Interview with Margie Poole at her home in Richmond, Virginia, June 2008:

I went to Edna's today to get a haircut. Remember she was Beulah's and my hairdresser. She had a shop in her home. She was in Penney's store you know, before she set up her own shop in her home. I used to take Beulah when we went to get our hair done. We would go together.

What I remember about Beulah is the places we went. I met Beulah at Elaine Powers which we renamed The Fat Farm. It was the same year I met Nell. We did all those machines that flopped you around and laid down on the bench and these wooden rollers would move over you for circulation and they didn't do no good. And finally they did more aerobics you know or the floor exercises and I think that's what helped us more but what was so funny was after we exercised for an hour or so we would all go to Hardies and have breakfast. Well, Beulah always was the coffee fiend. See I've never been a coffee drinker. But she and Nell were. I remember Beulah taking all the middle out of her biscuit and that's what Nell ate and Beulah would eat the top and the bottom.

You know when she found out she had cancer, you know I

took her there? And the doctor told her it would never kill her. This was after the biopsy. She went for the report and I didn't go in there with her. And you know we were driving back home and she just said Margie, I've got cancer. And I started crying and I don't remember her crying and then she said run me by Long John Silvers to get some fish to take home. I don't think it ever bothered her, do you think?

The first time we went to Radford, I drove. There was Nell and Claire and Beulah and me. I stayed with Edith and Fred because there wasn't enough room at Geneva's for all of us to stay there. And she bought a chest of drawers from her Aunt Florie and we went up there in the truck, I drove Joe's pickup truck up there to get the chest of drawers.

When I remember any of the stories about Beulah and Posey, it was always Posey that was involved in some situation.

Beulah was my friend. She was the person I went to if I needed to talk. I knew anything I told her in confidence would be kept to herself and she would never talk about it to anyone. I always felt if something was in my heart I could tell her and it would not go anywhere. A lovely lady.

We thought a lot of her. And Posey. They kind of evened each other out. Beulah was mild and Posey would tell these funny stories. I just loved him. You know Joe and I went to visit him at the nursing home and he took us back to his room and offered us some candy. He had it in a big candy jar on his dresser in his room.

Chapter 29

The Trips

Mama had never taken a trip to stay overnight, except to relative's homes, until she was seventy-one years old. We had never taken a vacation as a family. Daddy was way too tight to ever spend that kind of money for something so foolish as a vacation. She had read about places and of course had seen them on TV, but she had never been out of the state of Virginia. She had never flown in an airplane and had sworn that she would never, ever get in one.

She changed her mind because I had a free plane ticket as a result of getting bumped off a flight the year before. The plane ticket was getting ready to expire and I complained that I had no one to go with to use the ticket. To my amazement, she agreed to go with me and use the ticket. It was in October, 1990. She agreed to go if I would make all the arrangements and all she had to do was go along. All of this occurred one morning at breakfast at Bob Evan's; we had gone out for breakfast because Alice was visiting me; to this day I think Mama was being nervy for Alice's benefit.

There would be four more trips over the next six years, but it was that first trip that was always our favorite. We flew to Boston, rented a car and went to Cape Cod, Martha's Vineyard, Vermont, Bar Harbor, Maine and Burlington, Massachusetts. I picked Boston because it was only a two-hour flight, in case she hated it. I mentioned to the stewardess that Mama was taking her very first flight, that she was seventy-one and it just happened to be her birthday. After we were airborne, the pilots led everybody in singing Happy Birthday to Mama. She was embarrassed because she never wanted any attention paid to her.

At Logan airport in Boston, we picked up our rental car, a new Lincoln Continental. Her insistence that we have a luxury car was shocking. Doris had a Lincoln which Mama had occasion to ride in, and Mama said if we were going to be driving all over New England, she wanted to be comfortable. She had arthritis and normally wouldn't venture too far away from her soft recliner. Our deal was that I would choose the destination, plan the itinerary, choose the motels and take care of hefting the luggage, and pay for my own meals and she would pay for the rest. I consulted maps and tour books for weeks planning the trip. She wasn't particular where we went but she had bad ankles and couldn't do a lot of standing or walking, so I had to make careful choices.

It was raining when we left Logan airport, and it was in the middle of rush hour traffic in Boston. I was dealing with a totally unfamiliar car which had enough buttons and gadgets to launch a space ship, rush hour traffic, reading signs out of the airport through downtown Boston, windshield wipers, headlights and aggressive drivers. In the middle of all this, she said Can't you get some heat in this car, and I said If you want heat, you'll have to figure it out for yourself because I've got my hands full. When she pushed the heater button, a blast of air hit the windshield and it immediately fogged over. So now I couldn't see out of the windshield and for an awful moment, it was pure panic. I swiped the windshield with my bare hand and then I could see well enough to pull over. It scared her so bad that she wouldn't ever touch any buttons again.

We drove south of Boston to Plymouth Rock and stayed in a Ramada Inn that night. It was the first time Mama had ever stayed in a hotel. The room was $110 for the night and Mama thought that was too much. I agreed with her because this was late October and past the leaf season but we were tired and it was getting late. When we got to our room, Mama went to the bathroom and when she came out she wanted to know if that stuff on the counter in the bathroom was ours. When I looked, it was soap and shampoo and shower caps. She thought that was nice and from then on would take all of these when we left, even a partially used bottle of shampoo. And the next morning when we checked out, she also took a pillow. She couldn't bring her own pillow from home and having found one she really liked, she didn't trust that her luck would be as good in the next place. My mother had never stolen anything in her whole life. I reasoned that this made up for the high price they had charged for the room. She agreed but she knew it was wrong and it bothered her for the rest of the trip. I later offered to drive back to Plymouth Rock on the return leg of our trip to return the pillow, but we didn't, we left it at another motel the morning we left Boston to come home.

In our room at the Ramada, we were going to order a pot of coffee from room service until she asked how much would it cost. When I told her $3.95, she was floored and got really irritated that anyone would charge that kind of price for a pot of coffee. I knew what hotels charged for room service because I had traveled all over the country for my job but it was useless to try to explain. Later on in other trips together, she relented and we had room service coffee. She never said anything more about it but I knew she thought it was highway robbery.

As soon as we checked in, she called Daddy at home and told him that they had been worried about flying on a plane for nothing, that it was a piece of cake. Several years later, Harless bought a plane and got his pilot's license. She didn't hesitate to go flying with Harless. Daddy never did get in a plane.

And furthermore, she told Daddy, she was having a good time and she would probably do this again. And he shouldn't get drunk and burn the house down. And he shouldn't bring his muddy boots in the house on her clean floor. And he should remember to lock up the basement and the garage when he left (she knew he would be heading to the beer joint as soon as we pulled out of the driveway).

We had seafood platters for dinner that first night at a restaurant across the street from the Ramada Inn. Seafood was Mama's and my favorite food, battered and deep fried. She also insisted that any remainders of our dinners left with us in doggie bags. Thou shalt not leave food on the plate that you have spent your hard-earned money for. I asked her how she intended to reheat it. She said We'll figure out something because I ain't leaving this food. I had brought a collapsible cooler, so I filled it with ice and stowed the leftovers. The next morning, I went out to get some coffee to avoid the $3.95 room service charge. When I returned she had put the leftovers on top of the heating unit wrapped in a couple of napkins and had the heat on high. She happily ate leftover scallops with her coffee. I couldn't face eating partially heated, fried seafood but Mama could as she would eat almost anything to keep from wasting it.

We left Plymouth Rock and headed South and East toward Cape Cod. We took the ferry from Wood's Hole to Martha's Vineyard where we spent the night at the Harborside Inn, country-style furnishings with handmade dolls on the beds. Flowers still in bloom, azaleas of all colors, right on the water. Chimes from the sailboats coming into or leaving the harbor, me in seventh heaven on the water, Mama beginning to relax and not worry about every dime, laughing and talking about what she saw and showing more excitement than I had ever seen.

She remarked that she knew I must be happy because at least we were on the water. She was referring to my love of all things nautical, seashores, lighthouses, old fishing boats and old fishermen. She was really having a good time, I could see it. So I too began to relax. I had been so worried that she wouldn't like the plane ride and she would find everything too expensive and she might be bored. It turns out that she was worried I might be bored hanging around with her, restricted in what we could do, remarked that I should be off with a friend who could do things with me instead of dragging around with my mother. We were both supremely happy to be right where we were.

The next morning when we got off the ferry from Martha's

Vineyard, we were both really hungry and we found a Kentucky Fried Chicken right outside the ferry parking lot. I remember that meal even now, hot fried chicken and mashed potatoes with gravy and biscuits. She was pleased we didn't have to eat in a restaurant with high prices. I remember sitting there with her thinking it's going to be all right, this is going to be fun.

We headed West and North, across the state of Massachusetts, to Burlington, Vermont. Mama was navigator. She read the Triple A map, pointed out landmarks and studied the tour books to pick out a place for us to stay that night. We had no schedule and no reservations. We were just going to drive until we wanted to stop. We stopped and ate whenever we got hungry, sometimes picnics in rest areas, when we could find one because there were very few in New England. We remarked at how we had taken Virginia's numerous rest areas for granted up to now. And always the leftovers made into sandwiches from a loaf of bread we bought along the way, along with a supply of chips, candy and cold drinks.

We made our way through Vermont (the Norman Rockwell Museum), across Vermont and New Hampshire, sampling maple sugar candy and intentionally asking clerks in stores questions so we could hear their accent. There was still some color left in the leaves and sometimes I would pull over so we could have a good long look at the big yellow trees and the white birch trees that are nonexistent in the South. Each time we crossed a state line from Massachusetts to Vermont to New Hampshire to Maine, Mama would say Well here's another state I've never seen. Mama loved the Lincoln. It was pure luxury to ride in and to drive. I had finally figured out most of the buttons. Imagine being able to tell what the temperature was outside the car, from inside the car. I told Mama that when I got home I was going to go up to my jeep and give it a good kick in the tires after having been able to drive a Lincoln for a week.

In Maine, we went to Bar Harbor and the Acadia National Park. On the day we went through the park, we entered the main gate and started the one-hour drive around the park where the road was one way around the park. We were about three miles into the park before I realized I only had a quarter of a tank of gas. That's not much gas in a Lincoln. There was no way to turn around. We held our breath and coasted out of the park to a service station just outside the exit. Never again did I ever let the gas gauge get so low.

That night we stayed south of Bangor, Maine where Mama had her first lobster dinner. Again, the restaurant manager made a big deal out of it when he found out it was a first for Mama, putting on her bib and cracking her lobster for her. As became her habit for all the trips after, she asked for a baked potato and extra butter. We sat at a table in front of the window overlooking the water and the table was crowded with food and we felt like queens. Oh, Mama.

From there we headed South back toward Boston, spending two nights in Burlington, Massachusetts, where Mama had fried clams she would talk about for years after. Our last stop was at the John F. Kennedy Library where Mama especially wanted to go. She had thought John Kennedy was one of the great presidents and was really saddened by his assassination. I was a fan of Ernest Hemingway and was very excited to discover a large exhibit of Hemingway artifacts at the library.

From there we headed back to the airport to turn in that beautiful Lincoln and board the plane. Once we were settled in our seats for the flight home, I turned and, as a joke, said to Mama, Where next. She said Anywhere you want. You pick the place and I'll go. I said You're not just kidding and she said No, I mean it. I've stayed home all of my life and looked after you kids and your Daddy and scrimped and saved every penny and now I'm too old to do much but while I can still get around some, I want to go again. The hell with Posey, he will just have to pitch a fit about spending too much money. I've enjoyed myself on this trip and I've seen what I have been missing. So anytime you want to go, I'm ready. I said How far away will you go? What if I pick Montana? She said Anywhere is okay with me. I was stunned, but my mind started planning. We arrived back home and Daddy hadn't burned the house down and except for a pile of dirty clothes at the foot of his bed, the house was in good order. I don't think he had spent too much time at home, frankly.

The following spring, we went to Montana.

Chapter 30

Montana and Wyoming

*L*ate May 1991. We left Daddy in the yard at home, teary eyed, hanging into the window of the car giving me last minute instructions about not putting the pedal to the metal and to be keerful, which is Posey-speak for careful, and drove to Dulles Airport to begin our long flight to Salt Lake City, Utah. Doris had agreed to check on him every so often, bring him something to eat that he could heat up in the microwave, make sure he was eating and not hanging around in the beer joints and driving around drunk. Good luck. Mama issued her usual instructions about changing his underwear and being careful around the stove (he couldn't even boil water) and not burning the house down and not bringing his muddy boots in the house. He was pretty good about taking his boots off at the door but she and I both knew that he would be "down the street" as soon as our car was out of sight.

Even though I had been joking when I suggested we go out West, this was secretly where I wanted to go most. I had yearned for a long time to see the Big Sky of Wyoming and to indulge my cowgirl heart. We flew to Salt Lake City, Utah, rented a baby blue Lincoln and headed to Jackson Hole, Wyoming.

On the way, we got our first taste of the huge grasslands, snow on the mountains, miles of fencing, grazing horses, and lodge pole pine log houses of Wyoming. In Jackson Hole, everything was Western and green and gorgeous and we couldn't get enough of the view. We ate huge prime rib steaks and baked potatoes just as huge, with enormous amounts of butter on them. There were real cowboys with handlebar mustaches wearing dusty jeans and worn boots walking around town in Jackson Hole. The town square was an acre of grass in a park in the center of town with arches at all four corners made from elk antlers stacked and woven into arches. The antlers came from the Wapiti elk herds that came down from the hills in winter to range in woodlands a few miles outside of Jackson Hole. The antlers were gathered by the local Boy Scouts when they were shed by the bulls in early winter. There was an authentic stagecoach harnessed to four big Morgan horses to give you a ride around town. Breakfast was sourdough pancakes and eggs over easy at a place called Jedidiah's, named, I'm sure, after Jedidiah Smith, one of the original mountain men of Montana who contributed to the opening of the Western frontier, along with David Jackson whom the area is named after.

Everybody wore cowboy hats. Everybody. Men, women, old men, old women. Even the children. One morning at breakfast, we watched while a man in a ten-gallon hat was seated with his three stair-step boys, all wearing ten-gallon hats. They had manners, though, and took their hats off at the table. A few restaurants had a long shelf situated by the door for all the hats.

The next day, Mama stayed in the motel while I went horseback riding. The riding ranch was just a mile or two out of Jackson Hole. I was the only rider that morning, so I got my own private riding guide, a boy about seventeen years old. He was very friendly and helpful about getting me on the horse and as we took off down a worn path around the mountain and up the hill, he started making conversation and asked me where I was from. I said Virginia. He said Is that in Wyoming? I said Virginia, you know, the state of Virginia. On the East coast. Near Washington, D.C. Where the President lives. He said Oh. We rode in silence after that except for the horses letting go with some very loud and satisfying oat farts as we climbed up the hill in single file.

We got to the top of the mountain and from my perch on the horse, I got to see a good part of the valley of Jackson Hole, Wyoming, an important crossroads for the fur traders from 1807-1840, because six major trails converged in the valley. I had read that here fur traders from miles around met annually to trade pelts for other goods like blankets and tools. Looking out over the valley, I could imagine the fur traders' rough tents and campfires. I felt like a real Western cowgirl. Mama thought it was awfully funny when I could hardly get out of bed the next morning, and for several days went around laughing silently, mumbling under her breath about real cowgirls.

In Jackson Hole, we went through the Museum of the West, where there were life-sized wolves taking down a life-sized elk. A very large Grizzly, standing up, muzzle raised in fury. Hanging on a dress frame, a white leather deerskin Navajo wedding dress as soft as velvet. We bought Doris a large dream catcher, made into a square with the pieces held together with leather strips of hide and adorned with rabbit fur and large bird feathers, which we hoped were eagle feathers, but which we knew were not.

We drove North a short distance out of Jackson Hole to Moose, Wyoming where I had signed us up for a raft trip down the Snake River. We sat in the car waiting for the other rafters to show up and I looked at her and asked her one more time, Are you sure you want to do this? We don't have to do this, you know, but I think it would be fun. She said I've never been on a raft and never been on the water and I can't swim but let's do it. I said You'll have on a life vest and the river isn't very deep, but you can back out if you want to. She said No, let's go for it. Very modern words for Mama to use. Go for it. I laughed.

We took our raft trip down the Snake River and she made out just fine. We saw a moose grazing on the river bank, eagles nesting in a tall tree and otters skittering along the bank, watching cautiously as the raft floated by. She loved it.

That night we spent the night in Moose, Wyoming in a motel situated on the shore of Jackson Lake. The rooms were individual log cabins scattered around the edge of the lake. Everything there was made from lodge pole pines, the cabins, the furniture in the cabins, the dock by the lake, the boathouse, the restaurant. As rustic as it gets. When we checked in we got warnings that bear and moose had been known to come up on the porches of the cabins, so be watchful and don't leave any food outside. Being extra careful, I removed the bag of snacks from the car and put it in the cabin. That night in the restaurant, we ate looking out over the waters of Jackson Lake and we could see snow-capped mountains from our table. We were very, very content and very pleased with ourselves at our good luck in getting to see such a place as Wyoming. We wanted to try a buffalo burger but after eating it, we thought it wasn't a very big deal. Tasted just like a big hamburger. We decided to stick to prime rib until we got tired of it. We ate prime rib all through Wyoming and Montana and Idaho and Utah and never did tire of it.

That night in the cabin after we laid down to sleep, I heard a rustling noise coming from the other side of the room and sat straight up in bed and said Is that you? Mama said No, is it you? When I turned the light on, a chipmunk jumped out of the bag of snacks I had left sitting on the floor beside the dresser. I screamed and Mama jumped about two feet off the bed. The chipmunk raced across the room to the corner and disappeared in a crevice. After the bear and moose warnings, we laughed and laughed and couldn't go to sleep for a long time. Every time we would quiet down, I would say into the darkness, Is that you? And we would start laughing all over again.

On our way down the mountain the next morning, she made me stop along the side of the road and pick some yellow flowers to take back to Doris. We had seen these flowers growing in clumps on the ground with large daisy-like blooms, on mountaintops and walkways and growing by the side of the road, all over Wyoming for the last several days. We had remarked about how pretty they were. I said Mama, you mean you want me to take these flowers in my suitcase all the way back to Virginia? She said Yes. And that was that.

This started the practice of us bringing flowers back to Doris from every place we went. Doris collected dried flowers and Mama knew that she would like to have some flowers from

Wyoming. Tumbleweeds and sagebrush in Montana, cotton bolls from Mississippi, or unusual-looking seedpods and leaves from New England. It all went into my suitcase or the trunk of the car for Doris. She exclaimed excitedly when presented with these offerings and treated each as if they were gifts sent to her by a king. She put the flowers in vases or glass jars or tied them in bunches and hung them from the wall in her kitchen.

The next morning, we drove North through Grand Teton National Park and we stopped and looked and stopped and looked and looked some more. They were so grand and so beautiful. I relayed the history to Mama of how the Grand Tetons got their name. A French explorer discovered them and named them Grand Tetons; teton in French means titty. And they do look like grand titties sticking up into the sky.

By this time we were getting into higher and higher elevations and we began to notice it was getting harder to breathe, so we followed the advice from the tour books and did everything in slow motion. Mama was short-winded anyway so we kept reminding each other as we went along to slow down and take it easy.

We drove through Yellowstone Park that day and stayed the night just outside of the West entrance to the park. All through Yellowstone we could see the burned out trees from the fire in 1988, three years before. Everything we saw was more and more wondrous. It seemed like something more exciting than what we had just seen was always around the next corner. The grazing buffalo herds, the hot springs and bubbling mud, the waterfalls, the geysers, Old Faithful, buffaloes in the road. At Old Faithful, Mama got out to use the bathroom and I parked the car and waited. When I looked in the rearview mirror, I saw her weaving around, trying to make her way back to the car. I ran to her and she could hardly get her breath. There were no benches or seats for her to rest, so I turned over a trash can and perched her on it while I went and got the car and drove it up beside her. That scared her, not being able to breathe. She got over it but from then on, I made sure she didn't have to walk very far at those high elevations. (Five years later, in 1996, Mama's emphysema required her to go on oxygen twenty-four hours a day.)

Doris had asked me to take her a picture of a buffalo. Not just a boring, normal picture of a buffalo, grazing or something. She wanted a picture of a CHARGING buffalo, and clapped her hands laughing at the idea of me riling up a buffalo so he would charge and I could get her a proper picture. I think she figured I would do it. Every time we saw a buffalo on the side of the road, grazing, Mama would look at me sideways and grin and say There's a good one, if you want to get Doris' picture now.

When we got to our motel at the West entrance to the park, we had left Wyoming and were now in Montana. Counting Utah, that made three more states Mama had never seen. I had a few drinks in the bar that night in between doing loads of laundry in the motel laundry room. Mama wanted to stay in the room and read a book. Mama wasn't much on bars and really neither was I. I went there to pass the time between loads of laundry and to check out the locals. I listened to tall tales told by cowboys who were very much like the men in bars in the East. Same crowd, just bigger bulls in their stories.

Our plan the next day was to drive to see the restored mining town of Virginia City, Montana. I saw it on the map and it dawned on me why the kid in Jackson Hole at the horseback riding ranch had confused the state with the city. We got hoagie sandwiches and potato salad for our lunch at the deli on the way out of town. About halfway there we came upon a herd of cows, all over the road, on the side of the road and all up and down the road for a long ways. There were cowboys riding around among the cows and a Conestoga chuck wagon pulled over on the side of the road. I pulled off the road and we watched for a long time, trying to figure out what was going on. It looked like the cows had broken out of the fence. Finally I stopped one of the cowboys and asked what was going on and he pointed to another cowboy and said Ask him, I'm Argentina. I found out that it was a cattle drive, modern style, where they charge a bunch of greenhorns from the city to come out and rough it in Montana on a real cattle drive. They were moving about 500 head of cattle and calves from the winter pasture to the summer pasture, ten miles away. Half of the "cowboys" were from foreign countries. I stood there and watched them, imagining them as little boys in their homes in countries far away, watching John Wayne movies and wishing for a chance to be a cowboy.

We finally drove through all the cows and made our way to Virginia City, a restored Western outpost. There was an assayer's office for measuring gold, a couple of saloons with authentic swinging doors, and a bootery with a real cobbler, a post office, a schoolhouse and several general stores. Inside the stores were handmade Indian rugs, ten-gallon hats of felt and leather, silver hatbands, chaps, churned butter, penny candy that really cost a penny, and homemade ice cream. In one of the stores, we heard the story of long ago in the early 1900s when the sheriff of the town had been in cahoots with a bunch of outlaws. The sheriff would learn when a stagecoach with payroll and mail was due and he would signal the outlaws holed up outside of town. The stagecoach would get robbed and the sheriff would share in the spoils. They were found out though and a judge and jury sentenced them to hang. Their bodies were buried on Boot Hill just outside of town.

It was about time for our lunch anyway, so we made our way up to Boot Hill to have our picnic. There were nine graves, marked with wooden markers. Beside the graves were several large flat boulders which made a good table for our picnic. Sitting on the boulders, you could look around for 360 degrees. Tumbleweed and brush and wildflowers were right in front of our picnic area, green grass in the valley just beyond the hill, and mountains far off in the distance, snow on the mountains still visible from where we sat on our boulders. As we ate our lunch, we sat enjoying the sunshine and I remember that moment and thinking to myself…look around and memorize what you see, because I don't think I have ever felt that content and that happy anywhere else. Remember the green valley and the mountains beyond and the boulders and my mother and me, with the sun shining on our faces.

That was in 1991, before she had to have oxygen or found out about the cancer. I remember driving home that day thinking about how thankful I was to have shared that with my mother. And that I wouldn't ever forget that place and the serenity. It was many years before I shared my thoughts with her about that day. I wrote her a letter several years later.

Letter to Mama
Dated October 2, 1998

Dear Mama,

There is something I have been trying to tell you for about five years now, and I never had the courage. So I'm finally giving up trying to get up the nerve and decided to write you a letter.

It's about the time we went out West and spent the day going to Virginia City, Montana and back. It seemed to be a special day for you too, but there was one part of the day that was especially meaningful to me and that's the part I want to tell you about.

We had stopped that morning in West Yellowstone and bought some sandwiches and potato salad at the deli for our lunch. On the way, we encountered the cattle drive and later, when we got to Virginia City, we drove to the top of the hill to have our lunch. When we got out of the car, there was some dried-up sagebrush that you wanted me to gather for Doris. Then we unpacked our lunch and had a picnic on the boulders there, overlooking the valley.

Because we were on top of this hill, the valley spread below us in all directions and we could also see the town of Virginia City at the foot of the hill. As I sat there eating lunch, with the warmth of the sun on my shoulders and a breeze moving the tall grass, I was thinking that I must remember everything about this moment and this view so that I could recall it after you're gone. So I memorized as much as I could of the surrounding view. There were mountains in the distance, but mostly I remember how the valley sloped away from the hill we were on, and the green of spring all around because this was the first of June, spring coming later in Montana than we were used to back in Virginia. You could see out from the hill for a long way and this view will always be with me because I was there with my mother, thinking about how good life was and how much you meant to me.

We didn't talk much, but then we never did, being quiet with our own thoughts, because talking it up would spoil it. But all the way home that day, I was glad I had the picture in my mind and I thought to myself, yes, I have this and it will sustain me when she's gone. We didn't even know then that you had the cancer.

Now I'm going back to Montana without you. Maybe Doris and I will get to go to Virginia City (we did not). But I don't think I will tell her about that moment, because I'd like to keep it for my own, our secret time.

You don't have to mention this letter. It was just something I wanted you to know. It's so hard to say things in person, so at least now you know what I was thinking in Montana.

Janet

Mama called the night after I gave her the letter and told me how much it meant to her to get it. We never mentioned it again. I found the letter in the solid walnut box she kept her important papers in, after she died in 2001. In June 2004, I returned to Virginia City with my friend Joyce and went again to Boot Hill, where I scattered some of Mama's ashes around the boulders we had used for a table. I wanted very much for Mama to know that I had made the trip again to Montana just to put her ashes on that hill, so I said as we were going back down the hill, Joyce, when you get to heaven, will you tell her? Joyce said yes.

Chapter 31

Other Trips

For the next several years, we took a trip every year. By this time Mama and I had earned the names Thelma and Louise from Doris.

Orlando, Florida to visit Margie and Joe, where for the first time, she relented and allowed me to rent her an electronic cart to get around the grounds at the Botanical Gardens. She was struggling for breath.

A second trip to New England for more fried clams. This time we rented the Lincoln in Richmond and drove there. On the way, we saw the Liberty Bell in Philadelphia and on the way back, the Vietnam War Memorial in D.C. The war memorial brought Mama to tears, something I had rarely seen before.

A southern trip through West Virginia, Kentucky, Tennessee, Mississippi, Louisiana, Alabama, Georgia, South Carolina, North Carolina and back to Virginia. She happily counted off the states as we crossed each border. We spent a night at the Opryland Hotel in Nashville and the exorbitant cost soured her opinion of the hotel and the town from check-in to check-out.

In her opinion, there was no hotel, no matter how grand, that warranted $200 for one night. By the time we went South, she was on oxygen twenty-four hours a day, so we loaded fifteen tanks of oxygen of various sizes and a wheelchair in the trunk of the rented Lincoln. Our visit to Elvis's boyhood home in Tupelo, Mississippi, was the highlight of that trip for Mama. The small white frame house on a quiet shaded street was made into a museum, furnished with the Presleys' spare furniture, their dishes on the table, all of it reminiscent of the '40s and '50s. She walked through the two-room house and declared a kinship to Elvis because it looked just like the poor home she was born into. The trip South was in 1996. It was our last.

Chapter 32

Caring for Mama

Harless and Anne gave Mama a bar stool with a swivel chair so she could sit down in the kitchen and do her chores. From this stool, an oh so very useful gift, she peeled potatoes or washed vegetables at the sink, and fried chicken and tenderloin and made sausage gravy at the stove. She also sat on the stool with her head bent forward so we could wash her hair in the kitchen sink after she got too weak to do it herself. Doris or I came once a week to perform this small service and roll her hair up in pin curls or hair rollers, using the original version of hair rollers, the ones which had bristles in them. If the hair roller was applied too tightly, the bristles would cut into the scalp. We tended to her with patience and love and while we worked we talked to her about what was happening in our lives and the lives of the rest of our family. When her handwriting began to get shaky, we wrote the checks to pay the bills and balanced her checkbook. That segued into taking turns to take her to church on Sunday and to her many doctor appointments.

Recapping the last seven years of her life would be like

writing a medical journal. Mama had four different doctors, a general practitioner, an oncologist, a lung doctor, a heart doctor and periodically other orthopedic specialists or podiatrists. There was at least one doctor visit each week that I took her to and then follow-up phone calls back to the doctor's offices for lab results. Her medications were taken on a programmed basis, for example five days of one medication, followed by ten days of another and some were taken every day. All of the pills had to be crushed or taken in liquid form because she couldn't swallow due to the hernia in her esophagus. The list grew to thirteen medications in all. A list of her medications took up two typewritten pages, which was updated each time a medication was altered, added or deleted. I had typed up a list of her medications, the dosages, when they were prescribed and what they were prescribed for and updated the list when there was a change. And there were lots of changes. There were medications she took for certain ailments and other medications to counteract the side effects of those medications.

Once a month, the oxygen tanks were picked up by a service company and replaced with full tanks. We had to call the company to let them know when to pick up the used tanks.

On January 17, 2001, Mama went to Dr. James May, her oncologist, for the last time. She had been diagnosed with breast cancer in 1994 and had been on oral chemotherapy ever since. Had she been younger and not had emphysema, he would have removed her breast, but that was not an option, because she couldn't be fully anesthetized. Dr. May put her on oral chemo, and arrested the growth of the tumor. On her first visit with Dr. May seven years before, he had told her that the cancer was not going to be the cause of her death. And it wasn't. But she had continued to get weaker and weaker and on that last visit, he recommended hospice care because there was nothing more he could do. As I was wheeling her out of his office and down the hall to the elevator in her wheelchair, she said Well, they're sending me home to die. I was behind her pushing the wheelchair and she couldn't see my reaction. I crumbled from top to bottom, but managed to stay standing. What she said hit me so hard I couldn't breathe, but I had to get a grip, so I steeled myself, gritted my teeth and kept pushing. I wish now that I had just folded up and cried and let her see my real feelings. Why didn't I? I've asked myself that question a thousand times. I guess I felt that I had to be strong.

She died a month later on February 23rd. Nancy and I had been by her side for a whole week. It had started on Sunday when she was too weak to go to church. For the last year, going to church and the doctors was the only time she left the house. Nancy and I took turns taking her to church. She didn't feel strong enough to go that Sunday so I just went over to be with her. Monday was a holiday and I didn't have to work, so I spent that day with her too. She loved fried oysters, so I fried some for her, her giving play by play instructions like she always did from her recliner. There was nothing better than a fried oyster sandwich on a bun. When she was still able to stand and cook, she would fry oysters for herself and Daddy and would always fry extra ones and call me to say come on by and make yourself an oyster sandwich, there were some left over.

Her friend Nell called that day and said she wanted to come see Mama and would it be all right. Nancy and I had begun to be very protective of her and her strength because she would get worn out very easily. She was so short of breath that when her friends or sisters would call, we'd have to decide whether or not she was up to even a phone call. But Nell was Mama's best friend. There was no question that Nell was welcome. Even though I wanted to leave and give them some privacy, I couldn't because Mama needed her breathalyzer every fifteen minutes at that point. I was in a state of anxiety, petrified that something would happen and her oxygen tank would stop working. Even though we had backup portable oxygen tanks enough to last three or four days, there was always the possibility of having something fail and you'd be hooking up another tank in a panic while she was gasping for breath. Between the oxygen and the thirteen pills she had to take every day, Nancy and I felt responsible for her life, literally.

On Tuesday I called Harless to come home to help because it became obvious that she would have to have someone with her around the clock. Harless and Anne arrived on Wednesday and took over and I went back to work. On Wednesday we ordered a hospital bed so that we could set it up in the living room and have room to tend to her. She didn't see the need for that extra expense and she wanted to sleep in her own bed, but her bed was close to the wall and there was no way we could move about and tend to her.

On Wednesday night, Mama couldn't lie down and sleep because she couldn't breathe. Anne called Nancy and Nancy called me and the three of us gathered around Mama. We had liquid morphine on hand, supplied by hospice care. Mama asked for it and Nancy gave it to her. On Thursday morning, it started snowing and I went home to shower and change clothes. I called Wendy to tell her that her Meemaw didn't have long to live. When I got back to Mama's house, as I came in the back door, she looked up from her recliner and saw me and raised both of her arms off her chair as if to get up or as if to reach for me. But she couldn't get up, so I went to her and knelt by her chair. I laid my hand on her arm and I was too choked up to speak.

By Thursday afternoon, it had become a blizzard. Wendy left work in Springfield, Virginia about two hours away and headed to Richmond about 1:00 that afternoon. It took her seven hours to reach Richmond but she got there in time to speak to Mama and have her know that she was there.

We checked her oxygen constantly through the night and put pillows under her back to elevate her lungs. We took shifts, sitting by her bed. But there was nothing we could do to keep her from dying. She died the next morning.

I heard someone say the other day, if you knew this was your last day on earth, how would you spend it. Oh, Mama. I wish I had known it was your last day. I would have told you so many things.

Chapter 33

Her Children

$\mathscr{A}$ short while before Mama died, she told me she was scared of dying. I asked Brother Carlos from her church to come see her in the hope he would be able to offer her some peace. Later, at her Memorial Service, Brother Carlos told us that during that visit he had asked her to describe each of her children with one word. For me she used the word determination. For Nancy, roadrunner, capable of doing several things at one time. For Doris, she used the word particular. For Harless, she said he was the light of her life. I was a little jealous about that.

Because this book is about Mama, and not about her children, I have kept the material about her children short. There are truly enough memories for each child to fill a separate book. What I do need to say though is that I believe each child brought her an individual, special kind of joy. Each of us attained success in very respectable fields of work and were able to stand on our own. Each of us had experiences that she shared with us just in our telling of them. Likewise, each child brought her an individual kind of grief. Each of us had our own way of letting her down, trying her patience. After all, that is sometimes what children do.

She was steadfast, though, in her belief in us, bolstering first one and then the other to withstand life's trials. Standing proudly in the background when we did things right. Forever offering advice we thought we were too wise to need. Using old timey phrases and logic: sleep on it, it will be clearer in the morning; if at first you don't succeed, try, try again; all you have to do is try harder, you know you can do it. She would explain it to Daddy when one of us would win an award or be honored for something we had accomplished. Daddy, who didn't really understand at all, would be proud anyway. Especially proud if it involved a monetary award.

Unanimously, we loved and respected her and gave her most of the credit for raising us right. It was credit she deserved. We all thought she was the one who should have gotten an award. I think she knew that. I'd like to believe it.

Chapter 34

$\mathcal{E}$ulogy written by me and read by Brother Carlos at Mama's Memorial Service, February 27, 2001:

Images of my Mother

These are the pictures of my mother that I carry in my heart.

The image of her....sitting on her stool by the stove...frying oysters.

The image of her....picking beans in the garden in the early morning.

Her....sitting at her old sewing machine...sewing up the quilt patches...making a quilt for Albert and a quilt for Sydney.

The image of her....sitting on the bank...sobbing her heart out with relief...at the time I was five years old and I thought I could drive...and I climbed up on the tractor and drove it in a ditch.

The image of her standing at the stove...checking the pressure cooker, as she canned tomatoes.

Her arm…coming over the back of the front seat of the car when all us kids were little and rowdy in the back seat…with her hand searching to grab one of us kids to quiet us down,… and my brother pushing my arm out toward her hand, so she would have an easy target.

The image of her…when we lived on the farm…beheading a chicken…and then scalding it and picking off the feathers… then frying it up for dinner on Sunday.

Her….when I was about twelve years old…waiting for me to climb down out of the apple tree…where I had been reading a dirty book.

The image of her…hanging crinolines on the clothesline… heavy with starch…for her three daughters in 1957.

Her….on her knees by the bed, praying…when Harless had a football game.

Her….giving me money for college when I would come home on the weekend. Money she earned as a cook.

Her….at my wedding…in her new blue dress and her new blue hat and her new blue shoes…and her feet were killing her.

The image of her…standing at the sink…washing up the sausage mill…at hog-killing time.

Her….fussing at my Daddy, trying to keep him in line.

Her….sitting with me on a big rock…eating a picnic lunch… on a sunny day…while we were on vacation in Montana.

The image of her sitting in the passenger seat…reading the map and acting as navigator…as we drove all over New England.

Her....sitting in her chair...reading a good book.

The image of her pushing her walker all over the house.

The image of her face, when she talked about God.

And finally, the image of her sitting in her chair...with my brother and sisters and my Daddy holding her hand...as the end was near.

Chapter 35

To the Members

*T*he following is a letter I wrote to the members of the Buford Road Baptist Church, following her Memorial Service on February 27, 2001:

The family of Sister Beulah Wright would like to thank you from the bottom of our hearts for your outpouring of love and solace during our loss. You opened your arms and enfolded us with shoulders to cry on, words of comfort, and hearts filled with caring.

But most of all, what an enormous tribute to her, that so many of you came forward and expressed your sorrow at her loss. Each of your condolences was singularly meaningful, and taken together as a whole, was an overwhelming expression of love.

What joy and peace it brought her to belong to this church. Your unfailing faith and your hugs and prayers kept her spirits high as each week she came to this church to be uplifted. And uplift her you did. As her health failed over the last year, and she was confined to only being able to go out of the house once each week, she came here, to this church, to see you, the people who make up the church's heart. We thank you for loving her as you did.

Note: The letter was printed the following Sunday in the church bulletin. In her will, Mama left some money to the church and they used the money to partially finance a school for the children of church members on the grounds of the church. The school was subsequently dedicated in Mama's name at a Sunday service and was named the Beulah Wright Learning Center.

Chapter 36

Some Things Left Behind

After Mama died, we kids gathered to hear Doris read her will and what was in a handwritten letter she had left with instructions about certain things she especially wanted to give to each of the children. She left her pressure cooker to Harless, her sewing machine to me, the Christmas ornaments to Doris and some of the antiques to Nancy. Then we had to clean out her things. Each shirt or pair of slacks or sweater brought to mind seeing her in it. I held one shirt and thought she just had this on a few days ago. I know that she is gone but how can I bear it. We gave her clothes to her sisters, except I kept a blouse I remembered her wearing in New England and Wyoming. There were pieces of furniture she had given to us but of course we didn't take any of these pieces. Daddy still lived there.

Daddy was lost. Harless said Daddy, come live with me. Daddy said No, he didn't want to do that. But he said Why didn't Harless sell his place and come live with him? It made perfect sense to Daddy. His next suggestion was that we advertise to get "some old man" who could live there with him and help him out with his pigs. It wasn't a bad idea, really. I even looked, but couldn't find some old man.

Mama had a small chest of drawers in the living room where she kept all of her papers, catalogs, instruction manuals and a lot of odds and ends. When I cleaned it out, almost everything I came across told the story of her everyday life. I found tomato seeds she had kept from Daddy's tomatoes, dried, in plastic sandwich bags and labeled with the year, back to 1989. A copy of a repair ticket for brakes for Daddy's truck, made out to Strawberry. A little red book of Bible verses. Two packs of Skoal Bandit smokeless tobacco, mint (she started smoking when I was in high school and smoked unfiltered Chesterfields until she was about sixty-five years old and then she started using snuff). Canceled checks back to 1960 and tax returns back to 1968. A package of swine worm remover. Farmer's Almanacs for 1984 and 1985. A Best Attitude Award dated September 1982 from Elaine Powers. Two wooden clothespins, the kind without the metal spring. Six packages of shoestrings (Daddy always broke a lot of shoestrings in his boots). A key to an oxygen tank. A raunchy birthday card to Daddy from my Aunt Christine. The registration card for her 1973 Plymouth which expired in October 1998. A very greasy cookbook for her pressure cooker. Old address books containing addresses for people long dead. Two pairs of plastic sunglasses with visors which I had given to Mama and Daddy as a joke one Christmas. A program from Buford Road Baptist Church dated May 9, 1996 with a bookmark in it saying For the Best Mom Ever. A pocket calendar of Mama's, marked with the dates in 1999 when Daddy bred the sows and when the first frost had occurred.

A card from Jean: Happy Anniversary! Thank you so much for adopting this stray. Much love and blessings, your other child.

A homemade birthday card from me to Daddy, made from a sheet of typing paper, folded in half with flowers drawn on the front with crayons when Daddy was eighty-one. Inside was written: Roses are red, violets are blue, I couldn't buy you a birthday card, so this will have to do do. Love, Janet.

A Mother's Day card from me to Mama in 1990, dated a month after Mother's Day which said: Sarah and I found your card when we moved the bed, so I'm sending it, even though it's late. I know the suffering you have had to endure, so I celebrate Mother's Day every day. The time I spent on the cross stitch is only a brief moment when compared to the years you have given of your life in my behalf. I don't think I'm ever going to have enough guts to say these things to you aloud, but I want you to know that not a day goes by that I don't feel eternally thankful to have been lucky enough to have you for my mother. I am a whole and happy person for several reasons, but mostly because I'm strong. And all my strength came from you. Janet. (Sarah Rawlings was the little girl who lived next door and who hung out with me).

Cancelled checks to Wendy, Beau and Jason, $1.00 for each year of their lives on their birthdays. Beginning in 1996, the birthday checks were barely legible.

A small copy of her favorite poem, His Eye is on the Sparrow by Civilla D. Martin. It was worn and weathered and yellow:

His Eye is on the Sparrow

Whenever I am tempted, whenever clouds arise,
When songs give place to sighing, when hope within me dies,
I draw the closer to Him, from care He sets me free,
His eye is on the sparrow, and I know He watches me.

Chapter 37

Course

After Mama died, I thought back and thought to myself I wish I had had some kind of course to prepare me for when she got old and sick. All that useless information I memorized about the War of 1812 or the scientific symbol for magnesium. I really could have used some insight into aging. Perhaps they will change high school and college curriculums now that life expectancies are longer.

Mama visited her different doctors regularly and followed their advice. Daddy was a different story. He hated doctors. Or I thought it was hate until very late in his life when I realized it was fear, not hate. He hurt his leg once, badly, and we had to trick him into the car and into the emergency room. Cuts and bruises and even broken ribs did not slow him down. He would keep going, gritting his teeth and cussing under his breath. Three or four years before Mama died, he got impossible to live with. He had a cantankerous personality and wasn't easy to live with anyway, but it got worse. Nothing suited him and everything irritated him. Mama rattling dishes in the sink. The television too loud. The phone ringing would make him jump up and cuss. He had been irritable and ornery his whole life. We thought he was just being himself, only more so.

After Mama died, he was lost and lonely and everything started coming apart. His light seemed to go out. He stubbornly insisted on keeping his pigs and keeping his truck and keeping his driver's license. He was now eighty-seven. He began to get lost when he went too far away from home in his truck. He was really dangerous on the road because he couldn't hear horns or people coming up behind or beside him. Nancy went by his house almost every day. I went two or three times a week. Between the two of us, he always had something to eat and some company.

He stubbornly continued to drive. Finally we had no choice. We all agreed that something had to be done to get him off the road. When his license came up for renewal in the fall of that year, 2001, Doris convinced him that he had to get a required medical exam to continue to drive. Doris conspired with the doctor not to give him a passing grade. Doris told Daddy that since he had failed the medical he probably would not be issued a new license. When they arrived at DMV, Daddy got in line and handed over his expiring license. They told him then that he would not be eligible for a reissue. Daddy was devastated. That afternoon his blood pressure shot up to an unbelievable high and that night he had his first episode of wandering. He appeared at Junior and Betty's house next door at 3:00 a.m. that morning, carrying his shotgun. He wasn't going to use the gun, he just wanted Junior, who loved him like a son, to help him get rid of the dogs that were bothering his pigs. Of course, there were no dogs. Junior took him home and called Nancy. These episodes continued with more frequency for another six months.

Eventually he had to be committed to the Psychiatric Ward at Tucker Hospital because suddenly he was out of control and we couldn't handle him.

Chapter 38

Suzanne Lee

$\mathcal{S}$uzanne became attached to Daddy while she cared for him at Tucker Hospital. She was the nurse who completed the intake questionnaire when he was admitted to the Psychiatric Ward with what we suspected was dementia. Daddy was in a restraint jacket in the wheelchair, still struggling to get out even after they had given him tranquilizer shots in the Emergency Room, six in all, in increasing dosages since 4:00 a.m. that morning, February 19, 2002.

In the Emergency Room during the time since he was brought in by ambulance, Nancy and I stood watch beside him, trying to keep him in the bed. He wouldn't stay in the bed, climbing out of one side and then the other. Nancy and I, mentally in a panic, doing the best we could to control him and not let on how absolutely terrified we were. Posey Wright is not a person to be controlled if he doesn't want to be controlled. We'd had a lot of experience with his temper.

He seemed to be out of his head and did not want to do anything we asked him to, which was mainly lie still until the doctor came. He ignored us and resisted everyone else who came near. He didn't make a sound and he didn't have any expression on his face. Not anger, not fright, nothing. He just fought us to get out of that bed and get out of there. We had to give up finally because we couldn't keep him in the bed. The nurses and staff placed him in a straight jacket kind of contraption and finally he couldn't get out of the bed. But he never stopped trying. He was still straining and writhing to get out of the bed when they told us he would be admitted to the Psychiatric Ward upstairs. It was now 10:00 a.m.

He was moved from the ER to the Psychiatric Ward by wheelchair and they wheeled him into a room with two single beds. To get to the room, we had to pass through a large room where patients were sitting on couches or chairs or wheelchairs or were walking around. All of these patients were obviously very sick mentally. They stared into space, talked to themselves, slumped in their seats, cried silently, or drooled on their shirts. One older female patient used her cane as a leash and talked to her imaginary dog that was at the end of it. Never having been exposed to this kind of ward before, I couldn't breathe I was so frightened. We learned later we had nothing at all to be frightened about. They were absolutely harmless. At the time it was like waking up in a horror movie.

Suzanne came quietly into the room where we were sitting on the edge of the beds. Suzanne laid her clipboard on the bed and, talking directly into his ear, told Daddy she was going to remove the restraint. Nancy and I were horrified at this idea because we thought he would immediately get up and walk out, hospital gown or not. But we underestimated Suzanne and her skills with dementia patients. I thought at the time, well, all hell is going to break loose but she must know what she's doing. And she did.

She said We don't use restraints here. She gently began untying the strings, they looked like shoelaces, from the back of the wheelchair where they were anchored and asked him if he could get out of the wheelchair and sit on the bed. He said Yes, I can. He fumbled with the restraint, trying to help Suzanne get it off. He got out of the wheelchair, staggered a little, Suzanne holding him with her arm, clasping his hand from the inside. He calmly sat on the bed and folded his hands between his legs and sat there not moving. I could see the relief on Nancy's face and I was saying silently, Thank you, Thank you, Thank you.

He remained seated on the bed and allowed Suzanne to use a tool to examine his ears and mouth. All the while, she was talking directly into his ear in a louder voice than normal, but not shouting, with her face close to his. She asked him some questions, like Do you hurt anywhere? He said No. Do you feel okay? He said Yes, but my ears are roaring. He had begun to complain about his ears roaring some time ago, which the doctor determined was his hearing going bad and whenever examined by any nurse or doctor for the last four years, Daddy had brought this up as his number one complaint. I breathed a little easier at hearing him say this, thinking oh good, he's complaining about his ears. Good. Normal. Normal is good.

After Suzanne had completed her preliminary examination, she picked up her clipboard and sat down in the wheelchair, looked at the two of us and said All right, tell me what happened. I nodded to Nancy to tell the details because she had acquired an extensive knowledge of medications and symptoms while caring for her diabetic husband and she had a terrific memory for remembering the difficult names of medications as well as remembering the chronology of events. At this point, I was so scared I wouldn't have bet a dime on my memory.

But as soon as Suzanne picked up her clipboard and said, Tell me what happened, there was such a sense of relief, it was almost indescribable. Tears came to my eyes and I had to grit my teeth not to cry with relief. Here was someone who could help. Someone who wanted to help. They were going to keep him. We didn't have to take him home and deal with his anger and turmoil. He was in a hospital. They could figure out what was wrong. He would be safe. Like a child saved from a well who desperately hugs the person who retrieves her, my whole being hugged Suzanne with relief, even though I didn't move from the bed. Later Suzanne would tell us both that she saw the fright in our faces and the release of the strain once she took over.

Nancy began to relay the details leading up to his admittance, phrasing her words carefully and watching Daddy to see if he could hear. He didn't let on one way or the other, but he probably didn't because he was nearly deaf. Mama used to say that he couldn't hear himself fart, but I think he could because he used to look around and grin when he did it.

Nancy told Suzanne about the wandering at night, the loneliness after my mother's death, having to give up his driver's license, feeling useless, blood pressure being elevated for the past week. And the final straw the night before when Monika*, whom

---

* Monika is an au pair from Poland who later became part of our family when she married Jason.

we had hired to stay with him at night, had called to say that he was rearranging the dining room furniture. He had moved all of the chairs and the huge dining room table by himself, and finally tried to move the hutch with the dishes in it, nearly turning it over on himself. And she couldn't get him to stop. Neither could we. He wouldn't listen and he wouldn't calm down. Nancy and I had looked at each other and in that look, we agreed. This was over our heads. We needed help to calm him down. We called the Rescue Squad and here we were.

Suzanne listened and took notes and asked more questions and stayed with us a long time. She explained dementia to us. She described what it was like to have dementia. We began to understand. We began to add two and two. That's why he was always so irritable, seemed so miserable, nothing suited him, nothing worked right, took forever to say things, couldn't remember the right words for things, used words instead that sounded like the word he wanted.

Suzanne finished the intake interview and hugged us. I split up from Nancy and headed to my car. Made it halfway down the hall before I had to turn into a doorway and let go the sobs. I almost choked trying to keep quiet. I wanted to keen away my sorrow. Like you see women do in movies, I wanted to let go with one large wail. Oh Daddy, I'm so sorry.

We left him in her care for the next ten days. She was the one we called each day for a report on his progress. She was the one we sought out each day when we visited. She was the one who explained what was happening each time they changed his medication, while they were searching for the right combination. She wasn't the only one with information, but she was the one we trusted.

When he wouldn't eat, we suggested ice cream to Suzanne. She got it, he ate it. She was the one who called to tell us his urine output was dangerously low, indicating dehydration. She was the one we talked to about setting up an I.V. in the psych ward rather than transferring him into the regular hospital, which would have been disruptive for him. She was the one who said We're not really equipped to do that but, yes, we'll figure out a way.

Email note from me to Joyce dated February 23, 2002: Daddy seems to be a little better today. He is not as agitated and was able to feed himself some ice cream this morning. I don't know how long he will remain as well as he is today, but if he stays like this for a while, it may be possible to move him to a nursing home. But we're taking it a few hours at a time. He spoke of Mama this morning, saying she could be contrary when she wanted to be, and Nancy and I thought that was significant because he hasn't mentioned her name hardly at all in the last year and today is one year since her death. He did not realize what the date was.

Daddy gradually got better, but never went home again. Suzanne was the one who was there to hug him and tell him goodbye and keep well when he left the Psychiatric Ward and was transported to a nursing home. Her name was Suzanne Lee. She had been a nurse on the Psychiatric Ward for four years at that time. She is still there today, five years later, giving relief and comfort to the patients and their families.

Chapter 39

Southerland Place

$\mathcal{W}$e moved Daddy into the Dementia/Alzheimer's Ward at Southerland Place, a combination assisted living/nursing home in Southside Richmond in March 2002. The ward was locked twenty-four hours a day. Entrance and exit from the ward was through side doors which were equipped with combination keypad locks. The combination 1,2,3,4,5 was given to visitors. If anyone got within five feet of the locked door, inside or out, and did not enter the correct combination within ninety seconds to unlock the door, a loud abrasive blast from the security siren would emit until one of the aides or nurses reset it. From outside the ward, a visitor could enter easily, even with packages in hand. Inside the ward, the system was meant to keep the patients away from the doors and safe from wandering outside. The patients did not know the combination, but even if they did, they did not have the cognitive ability to remember it long enough to unlock the door in the allotted time frame. When visitors arrived through the side door, we entered the Day Room, a community area that was decorated with very nice furniture, comfortable chairs, loveseats, a large television on a stand in the corner and a piano.

We brought Mama's bed and chest of drawers and the sheets and bedspread Daddy was familiar with, along with one of their wing-backed stuffed chairs to put in his room. There was no need for a television or radio. He would just say turn that damned noise off.

He wanted to know what this place was. I lied and told him it was a hospital just like the one he had just left and he had to stay here a while longer to get well. He looked around the Day Room and remarked that this place must cost a fortune, at least $100 a month. I said Yes it does, but don't worry about it, you're going to get well. I could not tell him it cost $4,000 a month, actually, and was paid for by money he had in the bank from selling vegetables and raising pigs.

Daddy was given medications to keep him calm as well as drugs for mental stability, one of which was called Haldol. The dreaded Haldol. It made him crazier than he was already. Sometimes he was aware of things, other times not. Not long after he moved in, maybe a day later, we had been sitting out in the Day Room, and when we returned to his room, he said Janet was that your mother out there? I said No Daddy, that wasn't her. And gritted my teeth to hold back tears. And he said, Oh that's right, she was *cursumated*. He was trying to say cremated. My heart came right out of my chest and it was at that moment that I forgave him everything. I vowed to treat him with kindness and love and respect for the rest of his days, no matter how many there were left. Here was a man who leaned on the fence around his garden or his pigpens and gazed away and around him and I know he felt free. Now he was confined to a 9X12 room, a bed, a dresser and a walker.

The pain of seeing him that way was almost unbearable. When I visited him, if he was out of it, I was glad because then he didn't know where he was. When he was aware of where he was and cried for me to take him out of there was when it almost overcame me. Once he took his mattress off the bed and was shoving it down the hall on its side and whispered to me to get the door, he was leaving. About a week later, he remarked that he couldn't talk to them people in that hospital because they were all crazy. All of the patients were Alzheimer patients and when he was in his right mind they appeared to be crazy to him.

With time and medication adjustments, he grew gentler and would sit in the cutaway in the hall with me and sometimes fall asleep. He wouldn't always be able to identify people who came to visit him, but he always knew us kids, even when he was out of his head. He was never far from my mind while I was working during the day or at home in the evening. I would think about him waking in the night and not knowing where he was and lying real still until he could figure it out. If only he could just climb up on his tractor and ride on off down the road.

At Southerland Place, there were four tables in the dining room and four residents at each table. The chairs were pulled out of the way when a resident was in a wheelchair and the wheelchair was pulled right up to the table, like for Mr. Bill.

At Daddy's table, there was Mr. Reggie, Mr. Bill and Doc. The aides were all African American and they called the residents by Mr. or Miss, along with their first names. I never knew if this way of addressing the patients was a practice of the aides or a policy of Southerland Place, possibly some of both. Except for Doc. He was just called Doc. He had been the president of a bank and had a Doctorate in Commerce.

Doc and Mr. Reggie died during the time Daddy was there. Doc would walk the halls using a walker and would give speeches while he walked. You would catch phrases as he passed by and you knew it was from a speech he had given to the Lions Club. He was pretty far gone in his mind as far as being in the real world but he remembered those speeches.

Doc was a good looking man and you got the sense that he was popular with the ladies and was a gentleman. Nancy took to him right away and would give him a kiss on the cheek when going in or out of the nursing home. He would tell her that she was the most beautiful woman he had ever seen. In all the times I was there to visit Daddy that year, I never saw anyone there to visit Doc. Not once. Doc would sit at the table during meals and jabber away, giving his speeches. What he said didn't make much sense but there was enough that you knew he was a smart and educated man. Daddy would look up from his plate and look at me, shaking his head, and say in a perfectly normal voice, not whispering at all, Crazy as a loon. Mr. Posey had it figured out. When Doc died, the obituary was very long and filled with his accomplishments, so you knew he had children and they were proud. I guess they couldn't bear it when Doc didn't recognize them. He was seventy-one when he died.

Mr. Reggie didn't say anything at all. He ate his meals slowly and methodically, rarely looking up from his plate. He would smile pleasantly and return greetings when you spoke to him in the hall but you never saw him talking to any of the other residents. He would stop now and then when he was walking in the hall and look around him and then go on down the hall toward his room with his head down. When he was in his room, either sitting in his recliner or lying on his bed, he would say "Help" over and over. People passing by his room who didn't know this would pause and get a look of fright on their faces and look around wondering why no one was coming to help him and you knew they were thinking how cruel to just leave him there with no attention and him saying Help over and over and over. So you'd have to go up to them and explain that Mr. Reggie was okay, he just said Help all the time. Mr. Reggie died in his sleep one night and help finally arrived.

Mr. Reggie and Doc were small in size like Daddy, but Mr. Bill was very tall and rangy with large bones and large feet and hands. He had to be kept in a wheelchair because he was too big for the aides to handle. He always had trouble getting his feet under the table. He looked healthy as a horse, a handsome man, smiled a lot. He was as docile as a lamb. The aides had trouble getting his attention to move his feet out of the way. When he ate, he liked to use his hands and the aides were always putting his fork in his hand. He would use it for a while and then lay it down and start eating with his hands again. His wife Doris came to visit every day. She was as small as he was large. Together they had raised four children, all good looking and successful looking. They were all there with their spouses on Father's Day.

As a special treat for Father's Day, I had arranged for a Blue-grass band to play in the Day Room after lunch. The nurses brought some of the residents from the assisted living area so they could listen too. Some came in their wheelchairs and walkers. We dressed Daddy up in a dressy white shirt and his best pants and shoes and told him it was a special present for Father's Day. His face lit up when he heard the first notes of "Going up Cripple Creek." I know hearing it brought back memories of Grandpa Wright on the farm. Daddy danced with us that day and was more like his old self, grinning and shuffling his feet around to the music. He never picked his feet up but he shuffled them around faster than when he was walking and that's how you could tell he was dancing. The other residents clapped in time to the music and some got up and danced on their walkers, sticking one foot out the side of the walker and then the other foot out the other side.

The Day Room was jamming and the whole place got up and danced or clapped their hands when they played "Foggy Mountain Breakdown." Bluegrass music is an infectious kind of music, where you cannot sit still, you must tap your feet or get up and move to the music. We all did at various times. Betty who lived next door to Mama and Daddy was there. She loved Bluegrass music as much as Daddy and me and danced and clogged to her heart's content. Daddy tried very hard to keep up but fell asleep sitting in the chair after about an hour.

His favorite, and my favorite, of the aides was an African American woman named Karen. She was always so gentle with him and you could tell by the way she handled him that she loved her work. Daddy proposed to her at least once a week and told her she would make a fine wife and why didn't they just leave and go get a place somewhere. I think he might have been serious. Karen was good at settling him down and coaxing him to behave. But Posey Wright being Posey Wright, there was always a point you reached when telling him what to do, no matter who you were. Daddy knew that my name was in their records as the one to call when decisions had to be made about his care, or when other issues arose, good or bad. He knew because I told him. I wanted him to know there was a way for him to reach me. All he had to do was tell the nurse to call me and I would be there. One day in particular when Daddy was being ornery and not cooperating, Karen told him Mr. Posey, if you don't behave, I'm going to call your daughter. Karen said He looked at me with those beady eyes and said I don't give a damn who you call. But Daddy liked her and would stay out in the Day Room in the evening while she was working behind the desk and wouldn't go to bed until her shift was over at 11:00 p.m.

Seven or eight months passed and I learned to hate the sound of the security alarm going off, learned which aides could be trusted, learned I had to lean on the management staff for even the smallest things from cleaning his room to his laundry, learned that when I questioned Daddy's medications the doctor didn't hardly know how to react it was so unusual for family to get involved, and learned how very hard it was for the aides to care for these patients.

Daddy went through several phases during that time. One such phase was his fixit phase. There were many things he fixed, but none of them was broken. He broke them, though, in his effort to fix them. He would take his lamp apart or would try to take his walker apart and once, declared that the thermostat wasn't working and had the cover off of it and was "fixing" the insides before he was discovered. Nancy and I didn't know where this fixit phase came from at all, because he had never, to our knowledge, fixed anything at home during our whole lives. Each time he would take things apart, I would spend my visit talking to him while I put it back together. Invariably, I did it wrong, according to him. I removed a lot of these fixed things from his room and replaced them with new ones, not daring to tell him they were new. He would have objected loudly to spending that kind of money.

He gained a reputation with the other aides for fixing things. Karen bought him a plastic hammer and pliers and he was well-pleased with them and set about to fix a lot of things. Once he went into the Day Room and picked up the large television off its stand in the corner and was walking away with it, television still plugged in, when another aide named Patsy saw him and said What are you doing? This is broken, he said, and I have to move it over here to fix it. She tried to stop him. She said Mr. Posey, it's not your job, put it down. He said Don't you understand? This is broken and it's my job to fix it. Patsy said Well, you're fired. He looked at her, put the television back on its stand, reached into his back pocket for his hammer and pliers, pulled them out and threw them on the floor and said Well hellfire, I didn't want to work here any damn way.

In October, Nancy brought a cake and Doris brought ice cream and we celebrated his eighty-ninth birthday in the Day Room with the nurses and other residents. For the first time, Junior who lived next door to Daddy and who was Betty's partner, came to visit and enjoy the party. Junior loved Daddy like his own father and he had not visited before because he just couldn't stand to see him in the nursing home.

Daddy became more pale and white and stooped each day. He still said Hey when I showed up for my visits but he stopped wanting to go outside and he talked less and less. If I brought a loaf of fresh-made warm bread for him and Doc and Mr. Reggie, he ate and ate, but his only indication that he wanted more was slightly raising his hand in my direction. This preceded the phase of incessantly walking the halls. During this phase he spent most of his time while I was there and most of his time every day, all day according to the aides, walking down one side of the hall to his room and back up the other side of the hall to the Day Room. He said he was making rows in his garden. It put me in mind of a grey wolf I had seen in a fenced-in lot in Wyoming who paced inside the perimeter of the fence, going around and around and around, looking for a way out. The little spunk Daddy showed during that time was to run over the toes of one of the female residents who didn't like him and would come up and hit him hard on the arm. He knew she didn't know what she was doing, but he got his revenge on her toes nevertheless.

He fell and broke his hip so badly the following March that we had to agree to hip replacement surgery or he would forever be in pain, confined to a wheelchair. He had heart failure during the surgery and died. The last thing I heard him say as they were wheeling his gurney into the operating room was Y'all ain't driving this thing right, you got to drive it like this.

Chapter 40

The Handkerchief

Suzanne Lee, from the Psychiatric Ward at Tucker Hospital, had a cloth handkerchief in her hand when she attended Daddy's Memorial Service a week later. An actual cloth handkerchief like you used to see in your grandmother's Sunday purse. White, with little blue and pink flowers in the corners. She loaned it to me when I became emotional at the sight of her standing in the door of the funeral home. I used the handkerchief and somehow never gave it back to her after the funeral. I still have it. I keep it folded on my desk as a reminder of that time with Daddy. She loved Daddy, and she loved us, and I am so glad that she was there.

Johnny of a few words sent me a card when Daddy died that said everything there was to say about Daddy: He was one of a kind.

Chapter 41

Written and Read by Little Albert at Granddaddy's funeral

March 5, 2003

I want to take this time right now and say what a great person Granddaddy was. He was always fixing and taking things apart at the retirement home and at his house. He dedicated his life to his farm. Well right now he is in a better place with Meemaw. He probably is working on a farm or fixing everything in sight. A great memory I have of him is the farm. Whenever I see a pig I will remember him and whenever I look at a push cart, I will remember his smile. We will always love him and he will be watching over us. Thank you.

My grandson Albert was ten years old at this time. He prepared these words on his own and asked Wendy on the way to Daddy's Memorial Service if he could stand up and read them. He did so in a strong and projecting voice. Sydney, who was six, walked to the podium with him and stood by him as he read it.

Chapter 42

The Lady in Church

$\mathcal{I}$ went to church on Mother's Day at Mama's church. I went by myself and I wore a straw hat and the pretty flowered blouse that my friend Joyce gave me with a pair of white summer slacks.

Used to be, when I would take Mama to church, I would sit in the back at the end of the pew next to the center aisle. That way she could sit in her wheelchair in the aisle and we would put her oxygen tank on the floor next to her feet, out of the way. There was a speaker in the ceiling above us which was why we chose that area to begin with, so Mama could hear better, although sometimes when there was a solo the pitch of the singer's voice would be so penetrating that Mama would have to adjust her hearing aid. The singing was my favorite part. Boy did these people ever sing their hearts out. They sang as if they couldn't contain the joy in their souls. And the looks on their faces. Sometimes they closed their eyes and pressed their hands to their chests. To hear them sing brought tears to my eyes and I couldn't look at Mama.

On this day when I went back to Mama's church, I couldn't

sit in our usual place. They had it blocked off for ushers. I imagine they had wanted to do that all along but didn't because that was Mama's place. All of the people in the church loved Mama and fawned over her and always came to speak to her and hug her when it was at the point in the service to turn and greet your neighbor. They said she gave them inspiration because if she could show up as sick as she was then they could certainly make the effort. After she died I know the people were sad to look at that place with her no longer there in her wheelchair.

Another thing I liked about these people was that they called each other Brother and Sister. Mama was Sister Beulah. But the preacher was called Preacher Tony. Preacher Tony had been the preacher for as long as Mama had attended the church, about ten years. I had only known him about half that time, or as long as I had been taking Mama to church when she got too feeble to go alone. He had beautiful, thick, ash blond hair that he combed straight back from his forehead and it waved at the temples. I think he was a man who took great pride in how he looked. Mama told him once that everything in the world was okay as long as he kept smiling his beautiful smile.

So instead of sitting in our usual place, I took the last seat at the end of the pew a few rows ahead. I sat down next to a tiny little old lady with snow white hair. She turned to me and smiled warmly and offered me her hand while she moved over to let me in. A middle-aged man and his wife and several children were seated on the other side of the old lady. I guessed it was her son and grandchildren.

Not long after I sat down, I had to dig in my purse for a

tissue. I was filled with emotion. This was the first time I had been back to the church since Mama's funeral three years before. I had not come back in all this time because I knew how tearful I would be and I didn't think I could handle it. It wasn't sadness that made me cry. I knew Mama was finally out of pain and misery. It was just my love for her and the memory of how good she was and what I had felt like being there with her. And knowing that even in her pain and misery, Mama didn't want to die.

The little old lady shared her hymnal with me. As we sang the hymn, we discovered that we were both singing alto. Her voice a little weak but the notes clear and on key, mine hesitant with disuse and too many cigarettes and sometimes choked up with feeling. We both agreed that there weren't many of us altos around. She could see that every now and then I had to wipe my eyes. I managed to tell her that this used to be my Mama's church.

When it came time for greet your neighbor, Preacher Tony came to me and hugged me tightly and said I'm still smiling like Sister Beulah told me to. Right after that, Preacher Tony conducted his special Mother's Day ceremony where he recognizes the youngest and oldest mother, the mother with the most children with her at the service, and the mother traveling the greatest distance to the service. Each was called to the front and given a corsage of roses. There was a mother with five children and ten grandchildren at the service and a mother from Bangladesh. The little old lady beside me was the oldest mother at age ninety-two. It was then that we learned that the man was her grandson and the children, her great-grandchildren. I helped her out of the pew and into the aisle where her grandson took over to get her to the front of the church to receive a special corsage to commemorate the day.

At the end of the service, she told me she was going to save me a seat next Sunday so we could sing together again. I couldn't tell her that I was atheist and wouldn't be back until Mother's Day next year. But I was tempted to tell her that what she said was almost enough to make me come back, atheist or not.

Chapter 43

After

November 2003, Southern Shores, the Outer Banks, NC
I was playing a CD entitled The Healing, which a friend had given me. Violins and strings. Looking out over the water from the living room of the cottage on Eighth Street in Southern Shores. Seagulls quietly skimming the water. Sunset behind the cottage. Water a steel blue. The sky several shades of pink. The music and ocean fill my eyes with tears. Tomorrow I start to write the book. I am so thankful to be here. Oh, Mama.

May 2004, my home, Chesterfield, Virginia
Wendy called me today from her cell phone at the ballpark where Albert was playing in a baseball game. She called me during the game because nothing much was going on in the game. As soon as she got me on the phone, though, she let out a holler and said "Get him, Albert! Get him, Albert!" Then she hollered some more and about busted my eardrum. The batter on the other team had sent a line drive into center field

where Albert was positioned and Albert scooped up the ball and threw it to second base and got the guy out and they won the game. And then Wendy cried. And then I cried. It was one of those moments when you know that being a mother is just about the best thing there is.

August 2004, my home, Chesterfield, Virginia

Email from me to Harless, Doris and Nancy, subject: Faith lift. Dear all: Here's one for you. I was in a blue funk the first of the week. No earthly reason, just in one of those funks that come over you now and then. Didn't want to go out of the house, so I decided to clean out the dresser drawer where I keep my undies. It had not been sorted through for many moons. There was lace stuff in there from when I used to be a siren and we know how long ago that was. In the bottom of the drawer, I found a $50 bill in an envelope. The envelope said Seasons Greetings, so I knew right away it was Mama's Christmas gift and I had squirreled it away for some future emergency and forgotten about it. And I thought when I saw it, well there's Mama, come out of nowhere to give me a faith lift.

November 2005, Wendy's home, Fredericksburg, Virginia

Sydney and I were in her room sitting on her bed. Sydney was now eight years old. She was reading me a story on Thanksgiving Day out of a book from the library that had big words in it and she had never read the book before but she read the big words just fine. Mama's dresser and chest of drawers were in Sydney's room because Wendy had wanted to use them. Mama, you would be so proud of Sydney and how well she reads.

November 2005, my home, Chesterfield, Virginia

I am thinking about Mama more recently in terms of what has happened since she died that she doesn't know about. Things that I'm glad she doesn't know about. September 11, 2001. My retirement and Daddy's death on the same day. Hurricane Isabel. My cancer and chemo this past spring.

December 2005, my home, Chesterfield, Virginia

I was wrapping Christmas presents and was looking for a gift bag for Wendy's present. I unfolded one that had been used before and saved for reuse. Noticed the tag said From Mama to Janet. I crossed out my name and wrote Wendy's. Now it said From Mama to Wendy. Mama would approve.

February 23, 2006, my home, Chesterfield, Virginia

Mama, I wanted to write this down before I forgot it. Joyce came today. We are getting ready to take off on a trip together. My cancer screen was clear last month, so we are celebrating. I have several chapters of the book in draft. Joyce read them. Today it has been five years since you died. I got choked up just watching Joyce read. She laughed and she cried. Oh, Mama.

July 2006, Urbanna, Virginia

A Sunday. On a whim, I drove to Urbanna to have a meal of soft-shelled crabs. Just before I got there, going through West Point, there was a vegetable stand on the side of the road. There was a pickup truck backed up to the stand, with the bed of the truck full of corn. Suddenly I could taste the fresh corn from Daddy's garden, Silver Queen, with butter. Doris and I had a bet one summer as to who could eat the most ears at one time. I won. Thirteen ears.

I asked the man at the truck if the corn was local. He said I picked it at 6:00 this morning. I bought a dozen ears of corn, some cucumbers, cantaloupes, and tomatoes, both red and yellow (Mama always preferred the yellow). In other words, all the things in years past that I had loaded into the back of my car on a Sunday from Daddy's garden.

A little past West Point, there was field after field of green, green corn. Daddy would have raved about how pretty it was and what a good stand of corn it was. I was thinking that when I went around a bend in the road and up ahead there was Beulah Church on the right. You just never know when they're going to speak to you. How corny to say that but I felt like they were there.

August 2006, my home, Chesterfield, Virginia

I was going through several boxes of memorabilia from the attic. I found an envelope of pictures Albert had drawn when he was little. Two of them were dated Feb 13, 1999. Albert would have been five. One for Meemaw which had a picture of Albert with a red crew cut and Meemaw with a black box sitting beside her with a long cord to her nose which was an oxygen tank. One for Granddaddy with a picture of Albert with a red crew cut and Granddaddy with a pig that had a squiggly tail. In the same box I found a cancelled check dated February 1973 written in Wendy's eight-year old handwriting to Big Granny for $2.00. We were eating out at a Chinese Restaurant and to keep Wendy occupied, I gave her my checkbook and told her to write a check to anyone she wanted to and for any amount. She decided to send her Big Granny a present and wrote the check to Big Granny for $2.00. It started out as just a distraction for Wendy, but since it was a cute idea, we followed through and sent the check to Big Granny. Geneva cashed the check for Big Granny and I got the cancelled check back. I knew when we got it back that I would look at it one day and remember Wendy giving it to Big Granny.

August 26, 2006, Pulaski, Virginia

At the Wright reunion in Pulaski, Virginia, saw Daddy's brother Henry, now eighty and the last of Daddy's family. My cousins playing Bluegrass music. The banjo did its usual number on me and my eyes filled with tears. All of us were there, Harless, Anne, Nancy, and Doris. Later that same day at the Sutphin reunion in Salem, Virginia, my cousin Peewee said she had prayed for me while I had chemo. Imagine that. Her in a wheelchair and she found time to pray for me. Alice went with me to the reunion. Alice and I picked up Aunt Geneva in Radford and took her to what would be her last reunion.

November 18, 2006/November 24, 2006,
Richmond, Virginia

Doris' death of a heart attack and her Memorial Service at Bliley's Chippenham Chapel.

December 20, 2006, Medical College
of Virginia, Richmond, Virginia

I went to get a checkup for my pacemaker. Dr. Sheppard told me there is an electronic record on my pacemaker of intense heart activity on November 18 and 24. Doris' death and funeral are forever recorded on my pacemaker.

Closing

$\mathcal{H}$ere are some comments for the kind people, family or friends, who will read this book. Every family has stories. It seemed to me that our family had more than most. I have tried to tell them as true as I could. It has given me intense pleasure to remember them and write them down.

I realized very early on that the book would have to be as much about Daddy as it was about Mama because writing about Daddy would define Mama in a roundabout way. Writing about Daddy was a lot harder than I expected. He was a simple and absolutely predictable man whom we loved and respected. Please know that nothing in the book is meant to cast doubt on that fact. It was also because of his uniqueness that made writing about him fun.

I started writing this book in November 2003. In April 2005, I was told I had an aggressive form of cancer, Bcell lymphoma. In the moments after leaving the doctor's office as I tried not to sink under the burden of the knowledge, I had three thoughts: I'm really glad I spent those two winters on the beach…Maybe now I will lose some weight…I wonder if I will get to finish my book.

A gift to you, Mama.

Jan Watkins
Chesterfield, Virginia
October 2008

Dedicated to Doris Wright

$\mathcal{A}$ special page, dedicated to the memory of my sister Doris. She died of a heart attack at age 63 on Saturday, November 18, 2006, without warning. She loved Mama so much and I know what she would say about this book, like so many other times when she thought I had done something special, Janet, you've outdone yourself.

She loved all things Indian and collected sculptures of Indian chiefs and buffaloes, bows and arrows, pottery, Navajo rugs, jewelry, and even bought CDs with their music and chants. She collected artifacts from wherever she went and decorated her home with them. The dream catcher that Mama and I brought her from Wyoming was mounted on the wall above her fireplace. There were some of these artifacts which were not kept by the family or donated to friends and had to be sold when she died. The money from the sale of those artifacts will be donated in Doris' name to a girl from a Navajo tribe to be used as college tuition. Doris would like that.

Doris, at home, with Raisin.

Buffalo drawing from a handmade greeting card
purchased while I was with Doris on a trip
to the Navajo Indian Reservation in Arizona, 1997.

Photos

Cass Sutphin and Beulah Mae, on the steps of the house in Floyd County, Virginia, circa 1924.

Daddy's mother and sisters; left to right, Annie, Laura, mother Florence, Gladys, Dorothy and Dolly.

*On Flannigan's Farm, Mama and Daddy, Daddy holding Nancy,
Harless, Doris and Janet.*

On Flannigan's Farm, left to right, Harless, Janet, Doris and Nancy.

On Luck's Farm with the bull named Bill, Daddy, Mama, Nancy, Janet, Harless and Doris.

Grandpa Wright carrying a milk can on Wright's Farm.

Daddy coming home from work at Luck Construction, circa 1956.

Posey and Beulah Wright, circa 1980. The only formal portrait
Daddy ever agreed to. He wanted to wear his hat.

Wendy and me at the house on Warwick Road, 1970.

Us kids in 1976, Janet, Nancy, Harless and Doris.

Beulah and Posey's Grandchildren, Oscar Jr., Wendy and Jason. Not pictured: Paul and John Wright, adopted sons of Harless and Anne.

The Wright family, Christmas 1995, seated in front Janet, Anne. Back row seated Mama, Nancy, Harless, Daddy and Doris.

Meemaw tells Albert the story of Goldilocks and the Three Bears.

Albert with Daddy in the pigpens.

Glen and Wendy Michael.

Albert and Sydney.

Mama on our raft trip down the Snake River in Wyoming, 1991.

Uncle Fred and Mama at the Sutphin family reunion.

Daddy plowing his garden on Ruthers Road.

The Sutphin brothers and sisters at the Sutphin family reunion:
Seated front Christine, Beulah, Virginia, Phyllis.
Back row: Bud, Snowa, Geneva and Fred.

My friend Joyce. We were attending the 25ᵗʰ class reunion at Longwood University, 1989.

My friend Alice. We were attending my surprise 50ᵗʰ birthday party, 1992.

My friend Jean. We were attending the wedding of Alice's daughter Wendy, 1988.

Mama, in her picture for the Buford Road Baptist Church directory, 2000.

Sunrise on the Outer Banks, November 2003.

NAME GUIDE

Name:	**Relationship to me:**
Albert Petralia, IV	Grandson
Alice Gray	Friend
Beulah Mae Sutphin Wright	Mother
Betty Bartlett	Mama/Daddy's next door neighbor
Bud Sutphin	Uncle Bud, Mama's brother
Cass Sutphin	Grandmother Sutphin
Christine Sutherland	Aunt Christine, Mama's sister
Doris Wright	Sister
Dorothy Krivanic	Aunt Dorothy, Daddy's sister
Diane Lowry	High school friend
Edith Sutphin	Aunt Edith, Uncle Fred's wife
Elmond Sutphin	Grandfather Sutphin
Florence Wright	Grandmother Wright
Fred Sutphin	Uncle Fred, Mama's brother
Geneva Sutphin	Aunt Geneva, Mama's sister

Name:	Relationship to me:
Glen Michael	Son-in-law, Wendy's husband
Harding Wright	Uncle Harding, Daddy's brother
Harless Wright	Brother
Jason Beasley	Nephew, Nancy's son
Jean Wilson	Friend
Joan Tunstall	High school friend
John Wright	Nephew, adopted son of Harless and Anne
John William Wright	Grandfather Wright
Joyce Robinson	Friend
Junior Witherspoon	Mama/Daddy's next door neighbor
Margie Poole	Mama's best friend (husband Joe)
Nancy Wright Beasley	Sister
Nell Ellis	Mama's best friend (husband Ernie)
Oscar Beasley	Brother-in-law, Nancy's husband, now deceased
Oscar Beasley, Jr.	Nephew, Nancy's son
Myrtle Thornton	Aunt Myrtle, Mama's sister
Paul Wright	Nephew, adopted son of Harless and Anne

Name:	Relationship to me:
Peewee	Cousin, daughter of Aunt Myrtle
Posey Wright	Father
Sarah Rawlings	Little girl who lived next door to me
Snowa Lockhart	Aunt Snowa, Mama's sister
Suzanne Lee	Nurse at Tucker Psychiatric Hospital
Sydney Nicole Michael	Granddaughter
Virginia Franklin	Aunt Virginia, Mama's sister
Wendy Watkins Michael	Daughter